CONCISE (

TO

MAJOLICA

Text by

Rodolfo Falchi

Grange
BOOKS

Published By Grange Books
An Imprint of Grange Books PLC
The Grange, Grange Yard, London SE1 3AG
Published 1994
Printed in Italy by Litostampa I.G. - Gorle
ISBN 1 - 85627 - 577 - 9

ANCIENT ITALIAN MAJOLICA WARE

The origin of ceramics

Clay modelled by hand and dried in the sun undoubtedly formed the most primitive containers for holding precious water.

Later, the earth worked and baked by means of fire led to the creation of "terracotta". But this had the disadvantage of being rather porous and of therefore allowing liquids to seep away.

For this reason, right from the earliest times, man tried to find ways of making terracotta impermeable. At first he used a clayey-alkaline coating, but later the Ancient Egyptians used the technique of glazing, a very effective method which spread to the Assyrian-Babylonian culture and from there to Europe, which is still in use today.

The term "ceramics" derives from the Greek word "Kéramos" and includes all products created from moulded mineral substances which are mixed with water and worked by hand or on the wheel, moulded cold and baked in the heat of ovens. On this basis porcelain, grès and majolica are all to be considered ceramics.

The elements which are used to make these objects - water, earth and fire - are found all over the globe, and so we may say that ceramics is universal and fundamental to the life of man.

The primitive forms and decorations which were created originally for the most basic human needs, progressively evolved over the centuries in more refined and sophisticated ways and often gave rise to important artistic creations.

The splendid vases of classical Greece illustrated with mythical scenes are an important example. The decorative motifs were originally inspired by the sea and plants, arranged within bands decorated with accurately drawn lines and geometrical designs. Later, towards the eighth century BC, we begin to see the famous black fig-

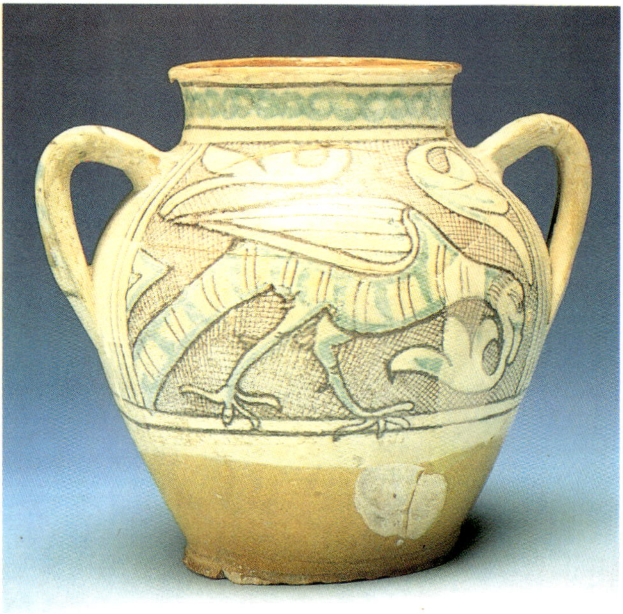

Two handled jug. Orvieto, circa 1380. Jug decorated in copper green and manganese with two illustrations set against each other showing a peacock among leaves on a net background. On the neck a chain motif.

ures painted on mainly reddish backgrounds. This technique was also used by the Attic potters who in their decorations represented stories and legends of gods, battles and funeral rites, depicting the figures with extraordinary movement and life.

Many later cultures borrowed from classical Greek pottery following their elegant forms of craters, amphoras and hydrias and their figurative decorations.

Archeological discoveries in Etruscan tombs brought to light a considerable number of ceramic objects with red and black figures. Only later did careful study demonstrate that these were Attic ceramics which had been inported.

Greek potters therefore made a contribution to the development of Etruscan artistic culture. From the Greeks the local craftsmen learned the use of a clear, lively design, which can also be seen in tomb mural paintings. Indeed, all Etruscan art was influenced by Greek models.

Apart from relying on Greece for their best pottery,

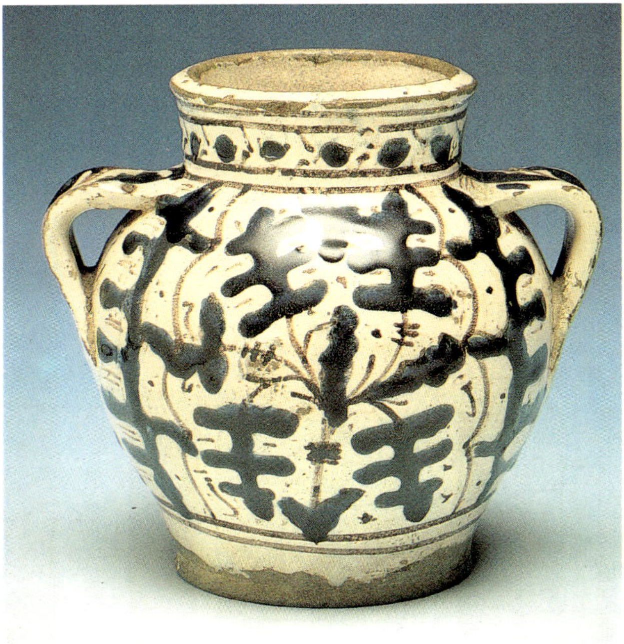

Two HANDLED JUG. *Tuscan, circa 1420. Jug decorated with oak leaves in deep "saphire" blue with borders. Lines and spirals in manganese brown. Band-shaped handles. Short cylindrical neck.*

from the beginning of the seventh century BC the Etruscans also produced their own. It was black pottery known as "Bucchero" and its appearance coincided with the height of the Etruscan civilization, which developed mainly in the centres of Tarquina, Caere and Chiusi. This type of pottery shows a tendency to imitate metal products, especially bronze, both in shape and decorative design.

Elsewhere in the Italian Peninsula similar ceramic products were also produced, especially around the Villanova cultures, but they never achieved the perfection and beauty of the Etruscan work.

Between the tenth and eleventh centuries rather unusual ceramic products developed in the Middle East, especially in the Islamic world. The artistic traditions of Egypt, Persia, Mesopotamia and Syria contributed to the evolution of a style of pottery characterized by its wide use of silicon both in the paste and in the coating. Such pottery was distinguishable by its use of material,

PITCHER DECORATED IN RELIEF. Viterbo, fifteenth century. Pitcher decorated in deep saphire blue in relief with manganese brown borders showing a hare among oak leaves and berries. Falling drops on the flared neck. Background dotted in brown, the dots sometimes grouped in triangles. "Squeezed" spout and rounded handle.

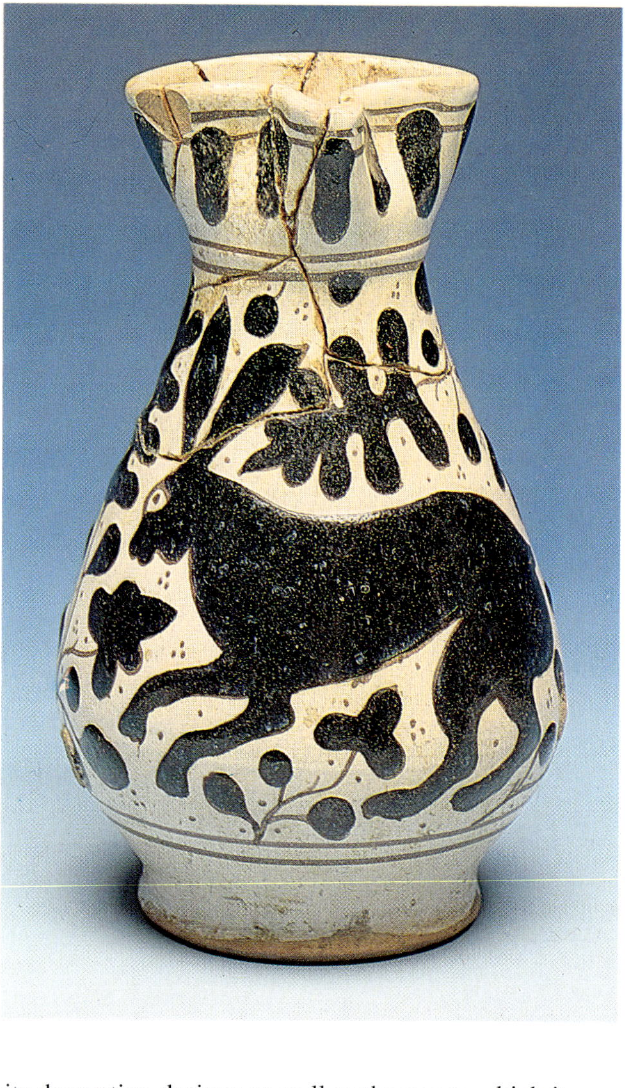

its decorative designs as well as the use to which it was put. One rather unusual technique which began in the Middle East and later spread throughout Europe produces a metallic gloss: this is MAJOLICA. An extremely thin film of changing colours covers the surface of the pottery, either completely or in part, forming an ab-

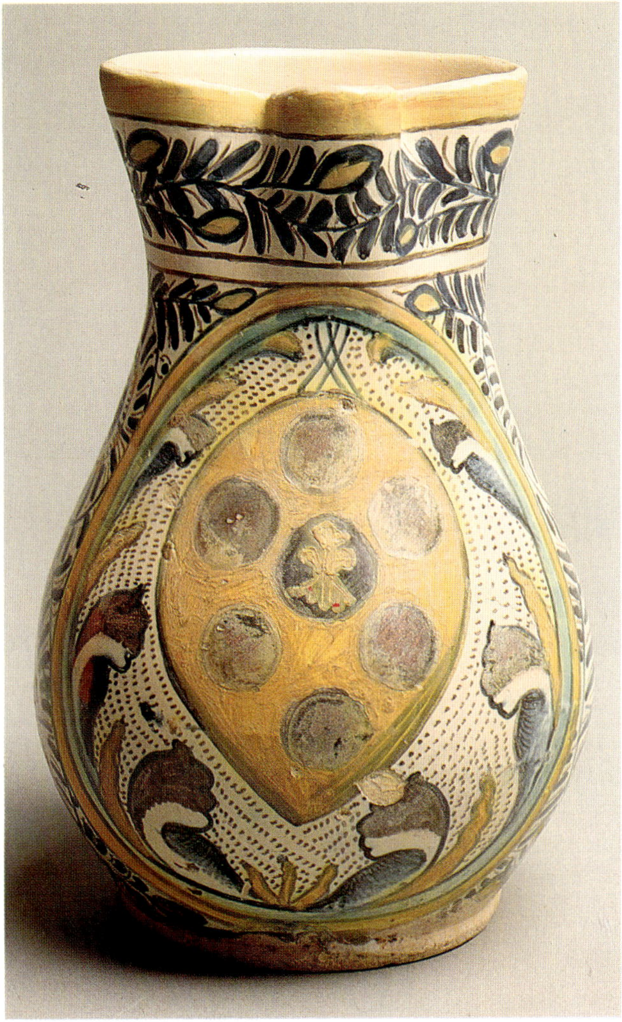

MULTI COLOURED PITCHER. Tuscany, fifteenth century. Rare Tuscan multi-coloured pitcher of the 1400s with the dei Medici coat of arms with seven balls on a dotted background and enclosed by an oval leaf motif. On the sides panels and floral decorations. "Squeezed" spout, band-shaped handle. Attributed to the workshop of Uliviero by Giovanni di Simone, Bachereto.

solutely unique decoration.

This metallic film is obtained by the reduction of an oxide or sulphide. The glossy pigment, which appears to have been discovered in Egypt, consisted of sulphur combined with silver oxide, gold or platinum, which produced the colour, and copper oxide which gave the

CYLYNDRICAL CHEMIST'S JAR. Florence, circa 1450. Multi-coloured decoration with curling gothic leaves among whirls. On the front, the chemist's emblem represented by a flower enclosed within a wreath of leaves. On the white band below we see the inscription.

gloss.

Having a different composition to porcelain and being similar to the most common pottery of the present day, glazed majolica was known to the Romans. It was imported from Alexandria as refined ceramic ware which was moulded in relief and characterized by a brilliant glossy coating.

In ancient times potters used a simple white coating upon which they scratched the outlines of a design. These are the "scratched" majolica objects having a simple design against a limited number of background colours, mainly pale green or yellow. The lead based paint served as a glaze on the objects, which were usually jugs, bowls and plates which might sometimes be embossed, made in shapes reminiscent of metal products.

Later on we find a powerful influence of Hispanic-Moorish majolica which culminated in the fifteenth century. The centres of production in Moorish Spain were Valenza, Granada and Barcelona, but majolica was also made in Andalusia and Castile where the methods of metallic-gloss glazing were developed to technical perfection. This type of glazing was imported from the Islamic East (Damascus, Cairo) and has been popular right from the thirteenth and fourteenth centuries.

In Italy glossy metallic glazes were produced in a wide range of tonalities, from bright ruby red, golden yellow, blue and mother-of-pearl. The greatest exponents of this glossy glaze technique in Italy were the Andreolis, a fairly well known family of majolica workers and ceramics painters active in the fifteenth century.

Undoubtedly the best known was Giorgio Andreoli who settled with his two sons in Gubbio around the end of the sixteenth century. It is from his hands that

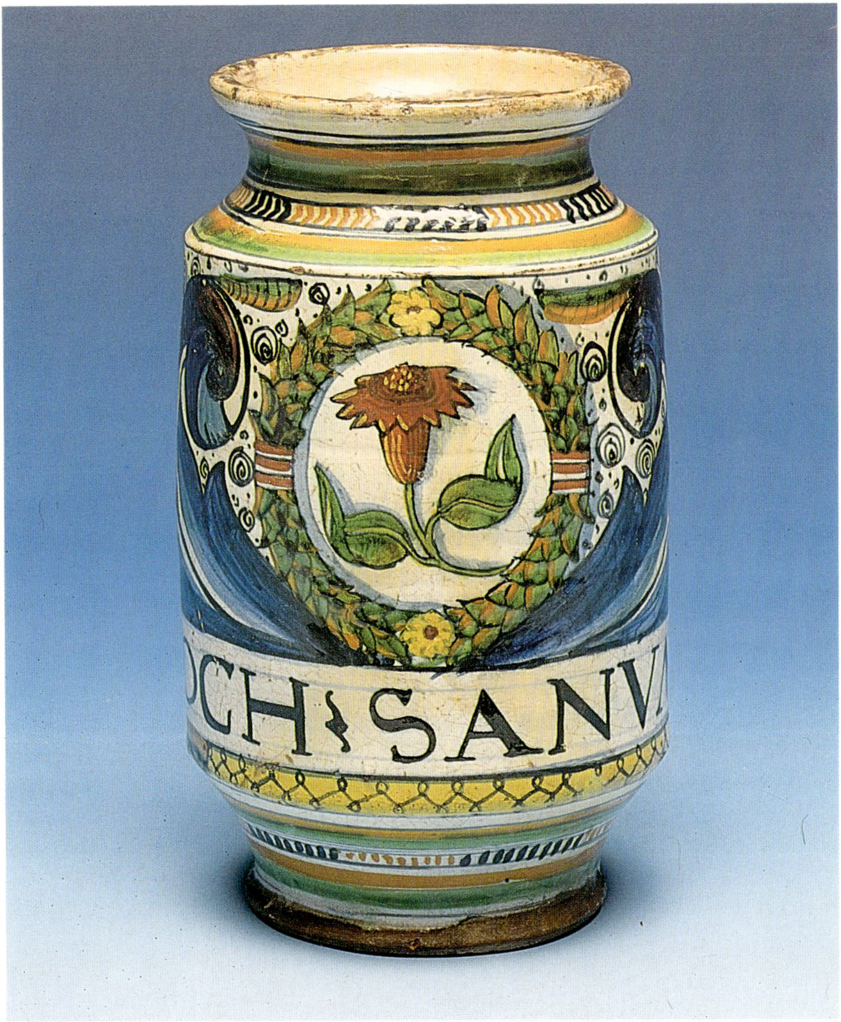

we get so many splendid glossy glaze ceramic objects in ruby red. It is well known that apart from the objects he actually made himself, Master Giorgio also superimposed metallic reflections on a great number of ceramic objects made by others. This fact led many majolica scholars to mistakenly attribute work to him, even though Master Giorgio always signed his own

LARGE FIFTEENTH CENTURY TUSCAN PLATE. Multi-coloured decoration. In the centre a bust of a young man in profile from the right with Renaissance cap on a background of leafy and flowering branches. The border is decorated with snake-patterns over vertical bars. The rim has a light blue stripe around it.

creations.

The maritime cities of Venice and Genoa, which had had close commercial and cultural links with the Islamic world right from the Middle Ages, had imported from those Oriental countries, and especially from Iznik, a great quantity of ceramic products whose forms, decorative designs and technique greatly influenced the production of majolica both in Venice and Genoa as well as in Italy in general.

The presence of Islamic pottery in Italy is also confirmed by excavations in which fragments have been found which date back to the twelfth and thirteenth centuries. It was not by chance that Italian ceramics moved towards two techniques of coating which developed from Oriental methods. The first of these was the use of lead based paint and the second was the use of a stanniferous glaze, or in other words majolica.

Oriental art expressed itself over such a vast span of time and territory that it influenced the applied arts of a great number of civilizations. This is particularly true of miniatures, bronzes, carpets and ceramics. Characteristic of Islamic art are distinctive decorative designs involving arabesques in which a motif is repeated and varied in an infinite variety of ways. And we can observe such features in various forms in a great many European products including many Renaissance furnishings.

It was customary to apply this term (arabesque or rabesque) even to "grotesque" decorative designs, and not only to sixteenth century majolica but also to murals, whose polychrome and geometrical designs exclude any representation of living creatures. Some of the most typical decorations of the late Italian Renaissance are arabesques formed by flowers and branching foliage.

One of the characteristics of Muslim arabesques is

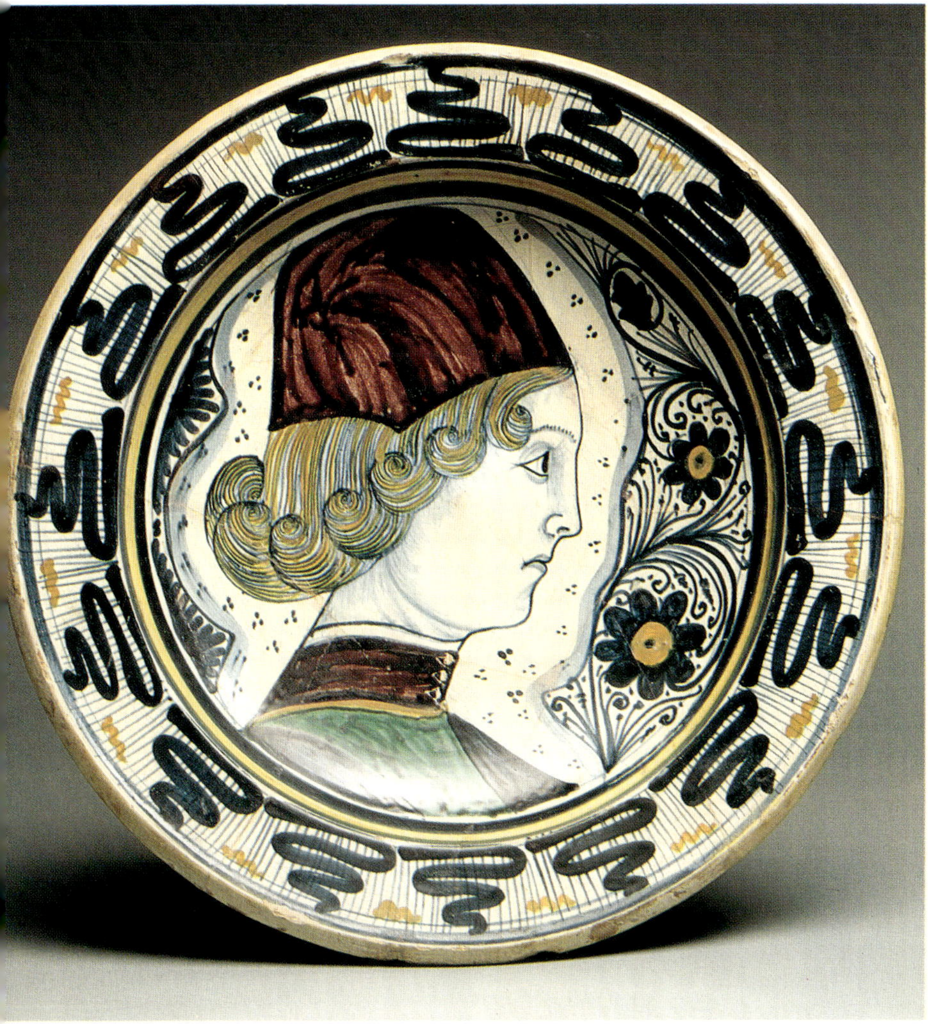

that of never representing man, in that man is not considered to be at the centre of creation.

Other types of Oriental decoration applied to ceramics which later spread to Europe, were "scratched" majolica and Majoica painted "under the glaze".

It seems that the "scratched under the glaze ceramics" come from Oriental methods of using clear paste

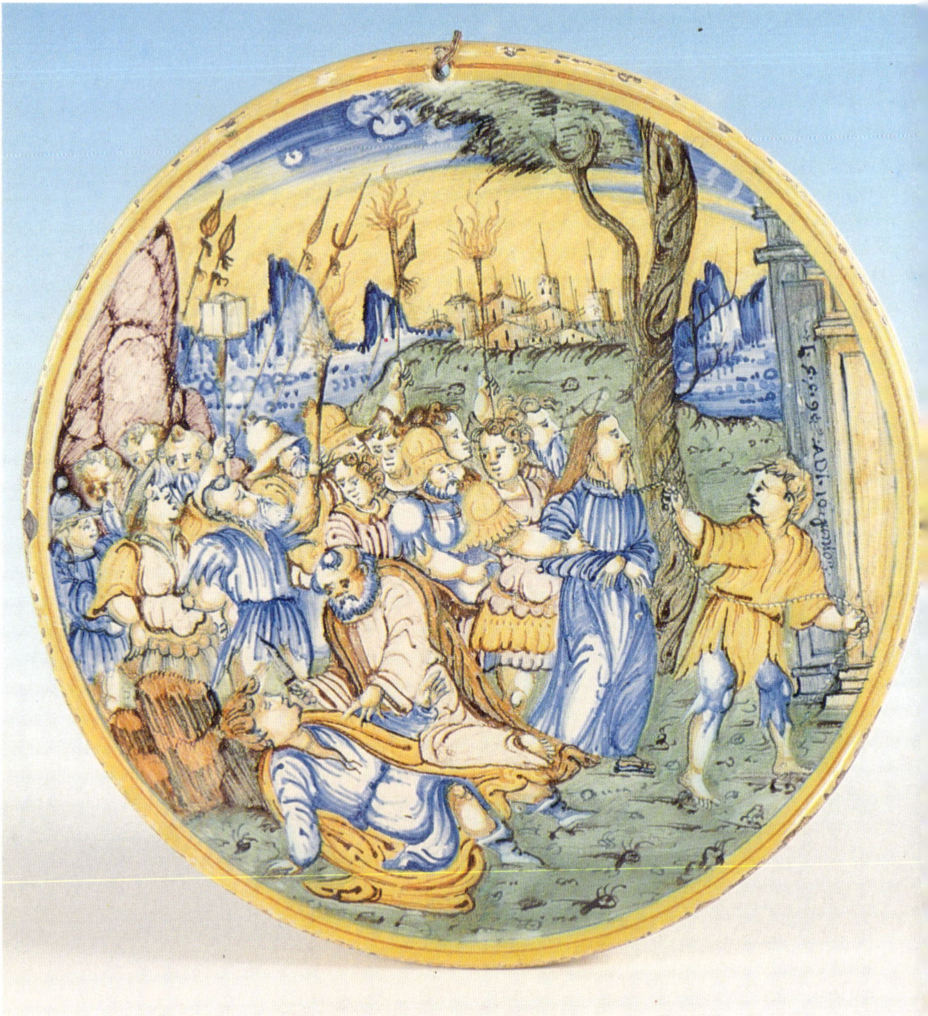

Chinese porcelain painted in a single colour, either sea green, jade green or turquoise. This ceramic ware was decorated beneath the colour with vegetable or animal motifs which were either engraved in the silicon paste or else made in relief.

The technique of decoration beneath the glaze spread contemporaneously in Persia and in Turkey. The polychrome decorations were applied to pre-baked paste, then the surface was covered by transparent glaze or else coloured turquoise, yellow, brown, pink and blue. This method of working was widely taken up again in Italian and French majolica production in the eighteenth century.

The fifteenth century and mrdieval majolica

In the thirteenth century there appeared the first examples of Italian "majolica" in which the glaze was made white and opaque by the addition of tin oxide. This technique, too, just like that of the metallic gloss, comes from the Islamic world. And majolica ware was classified by scholars in the Middle Ages into subdivisions of "FAMILIES".

Thus we have the green Florentine family, which began to appear towards the fourteenth century both in Florence and in the surrounding districts. The decorations on this majolica ware are dark brown on a green background, while in the centre of plates and bowls there are sketches of coats of arms, family emblems, lion flag holders, knights in armour and slender maidens. The "green family" was produced right up to the sixteenth century, but already in the mid 1400s a few Florentine majolica crafstmen had begun to introduce into their "CEREMONIAL" plates (used only for decoration) figures and decorations taken from the most celebrated painters of the day. Thus it was Florence, the capital of the Renaissance, which broke the decorative traditions of the late Middle Ages in majolica craftsmanship too, moving towards a more fluid and pictorial way of decorating ceramics.

Belonging to this transitional period in majolica decoration is the extraordinary work of the celebrated Della Robbia family. However, their splendid "glazed terra-

VOTIVE PLAQUE. Cafaggiolo, sixteenth century. Round, religious plaque from a factory in Cafaggiolo. multi-coloured decoration with scenes showing the mocking of Christ. The inscription on a column on the right records the date "1559 ADI.10 gunio". On the back a plain blue decoration.

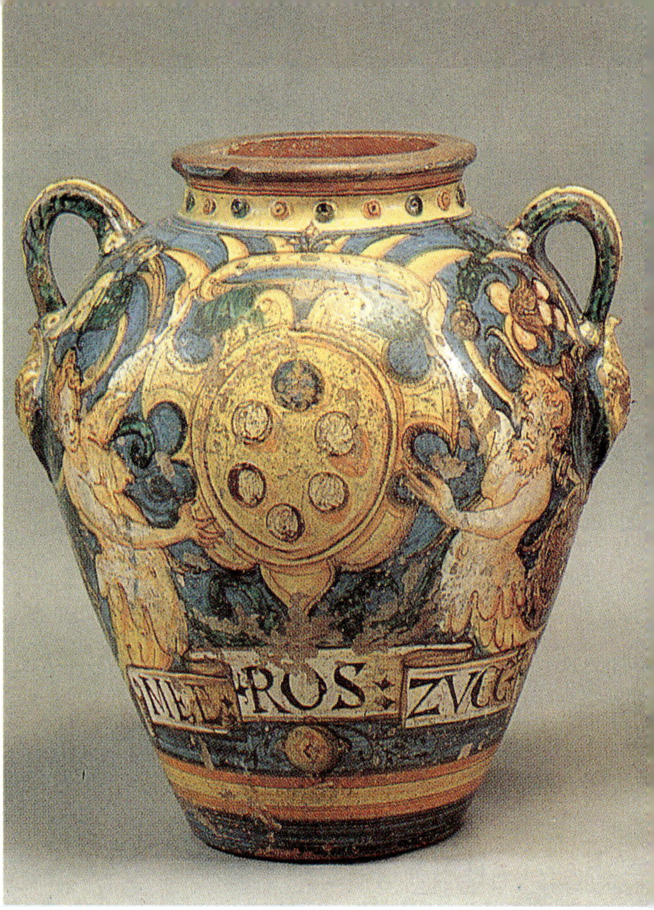

cotta", which decorate Florentine churches and ancient palaces, belong in our opinion more to the field of scupture and relief than to majolica work.

In Tuscany, Umbria, Lazio and Romagna we find the saphire- blue relief "FAMILY" whose name derives from the predominant dark blue colour of the decorations. These decorations represent stylized animals, emblems, fantastic human figures, and especially oak leaves in all their possible graphic forms.

Other "FAMILIES" classified by the ceramics scholar Ballardini are: the "floreal gothic", whose principal characteristic is a trail of curled leaves like a vine

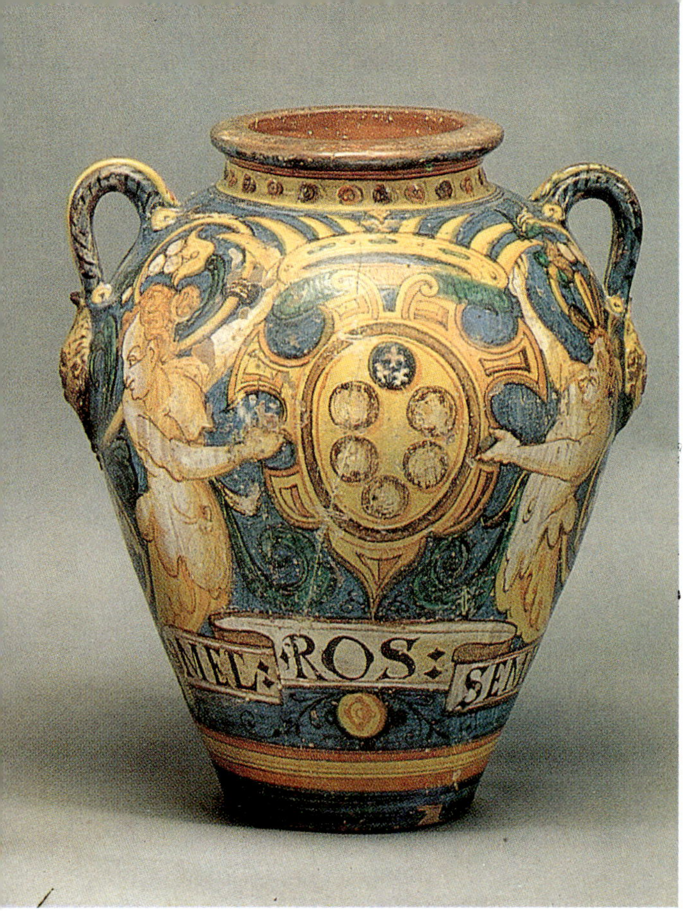

Pair of large jars. Cafaggiolo 1570. Multi-coloured decoration with the dei Medici coat of arms supported by mermaids and tritons. On the back a flowered vase among festoons, spirals and masks surmounted by an animal. Two rope-like handles with the lower join in the form of satyre's heads. The two jars contained an infusion of "lemon balm", a ple asant-smelling herbacious plant with large hairy leaves. They were used in ancient times for medicinal purposes.

around the edge of a plate or chemist's jug; the "peacock feather family" which comes originally from the Orient and which symbolizes the eternal life of the soul; the "Persian palm", which is also Oriental and derives from the designs of the ancient carpets which were imported in large numbers from Persia; finally there is the "Hispanic-Moorish" family, which came to Italy from the Iberian Peninsular.

In the fifteenth century majolica art, like many other important art forms, stagnated. And yet at the same time we also see stylistic and technical development, and the structural forms of majolica ware evolve so that

PAIR OF CHEMIST'S JARS. Montelupo, middle of the sixteenth century. The two pieces are decorated with the gothic leaf motif in deep blue, pale blue, with shading in manganese and small two-part leaves in orange and green.

we get plates of different sizes and chemist's jars of the most varied kind, even if at the same time the more traditional jugs and bowls continue to be produced in large numbers.

THE SIXTEENTH CENTURY: THE GOLDEN AGE OF ITALIAN MAJOLICA

There is no doubt that the sixteenth century in Italy produced the finest majolica ware of all times. Ceramics centres such as Faenza, Urbino, Deruta, Montelupo, Cafaggiolo, Pesaro and many others owe their fame to the majolica production of the 1500s.

The splendid Renaissance palaces which sprang up almost everwhere had facades which had been designed by famous architects of the time. Consequently, the interiors, too, needed furnishings of equal artistic merit. The beautiful and richly worked sideboards, which made such a fine display in the salons of noble families, were adorned with expensive cloths, gold and silver furnishings and refined ceremonial ceramics as a tangible demonstration of the economic power acquired by the master of the house.

In this revived interest in furnishings (a status symbol for the country gentleman) pottery is no longer considered a "minor art", but on the contrary an independent form of artistic expression of the highest value, as witnessed by the exceptional nature of the work of the Della Robbia family.

Whole families of majolica craftsmen, who are quite rightly a part of the history of art, now employed designs taken from the paintings of Raffaello and Perugino on enormous "ceremonial" plates and monumental centre table vases and trays.

In the opinion of Bernard Rackman, the English ceramics scholar, painting on majolica in the sixteenth

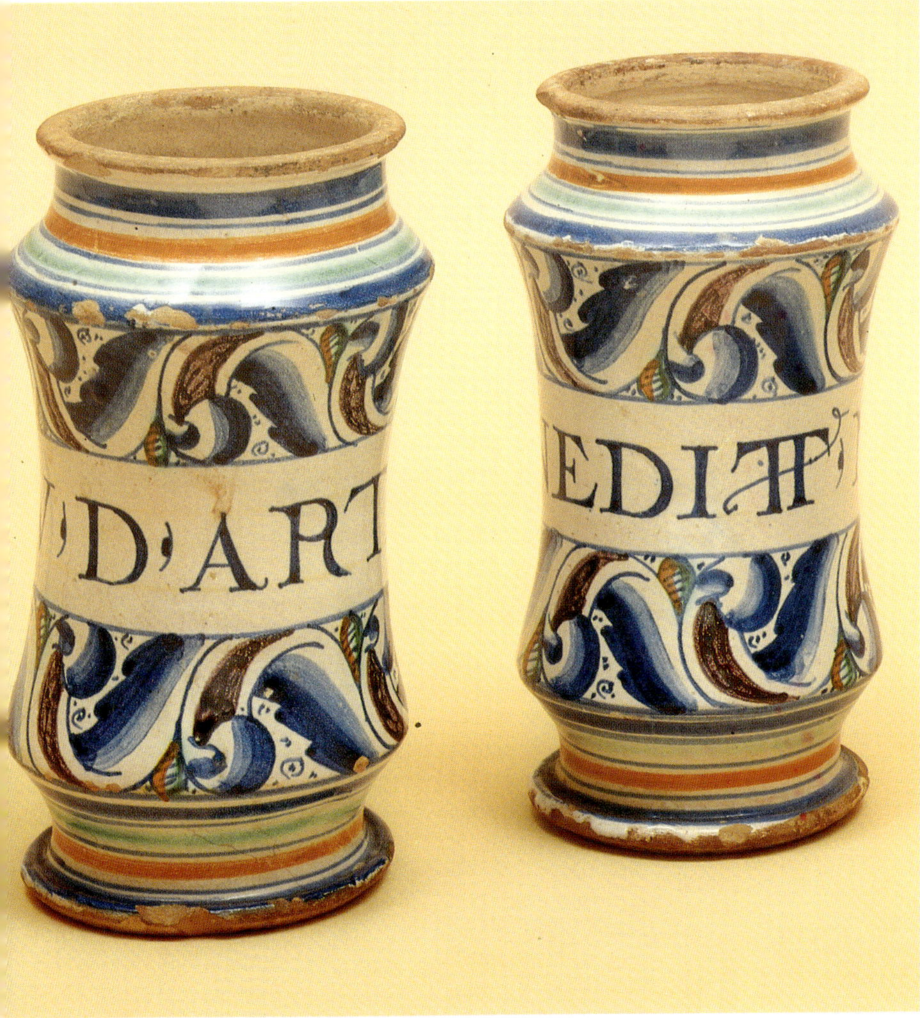

century rose to such a level as to be practised as an end in itself. At Italian courts, and especially that of the de'Medici family, there was a fashion for collecting majolica decorated with the faces of beautiful women, Biblical and religious subjects of exceptional pictorial quality, noble coats of arms, Raphaelesques and grotesques which completely cover drink coolers, goblets,

FRIENDSHIP PLATE. Faenza, beginning of the 1500s. Typical of Renaissance production in Faenza are the decorations known as "Beauty" and "Friendship". It was the custom to give these unusual majolica pieces at engagements or when agreements were made between people.

plaques, ink stands and plates.

In Renaissance Florence, then, most majolica production was concentrated in surrounding areas like Montelupo and Cafaggiolo, centres with excellent clay deposits. And here, under the auspices of noble families such as the dei Medicis, ceramic ware of the highest quality was produced.

Montelupo

Montelupo is an ancient ceramics centre situated between Florence and Pisa noted for its glazed terracotta and, in the 1500s, for its majolica.

Products dating back to the sixteenth century which were made in the workshops of Montelupo have been found in Liguria, Holland, England and on the African coast. Indeed the commercial outlet for its majolica was possible because of the trade that Florentine merchants had with the largest maritime cities of the time. Montelupo was already noted for its glazed terracotta in the fifteenth century. This pottery was mainly in managanese brown and copper green and decorated with flowers and arabesques in relief, figures, inscriptions and landscapes.

In 1506 a few potters from Montelupo founded a centre for the production of majolica at Cafaggiolo in order to meet the needs of the dei Medici family. Among these was a certain Fattorini, who was a highly talented potter and decorator.

A document from 1490 reveals that Francesco Antinori of Florence contracted to purchase the entire production of twenty three potters from Montelupo at a fixed price. This event proves that majolica from Montelupo was principally made for export. A similar example is that of Deruta, a small town with an enormous production of ceramics made possible by the financial support of rich merchants.

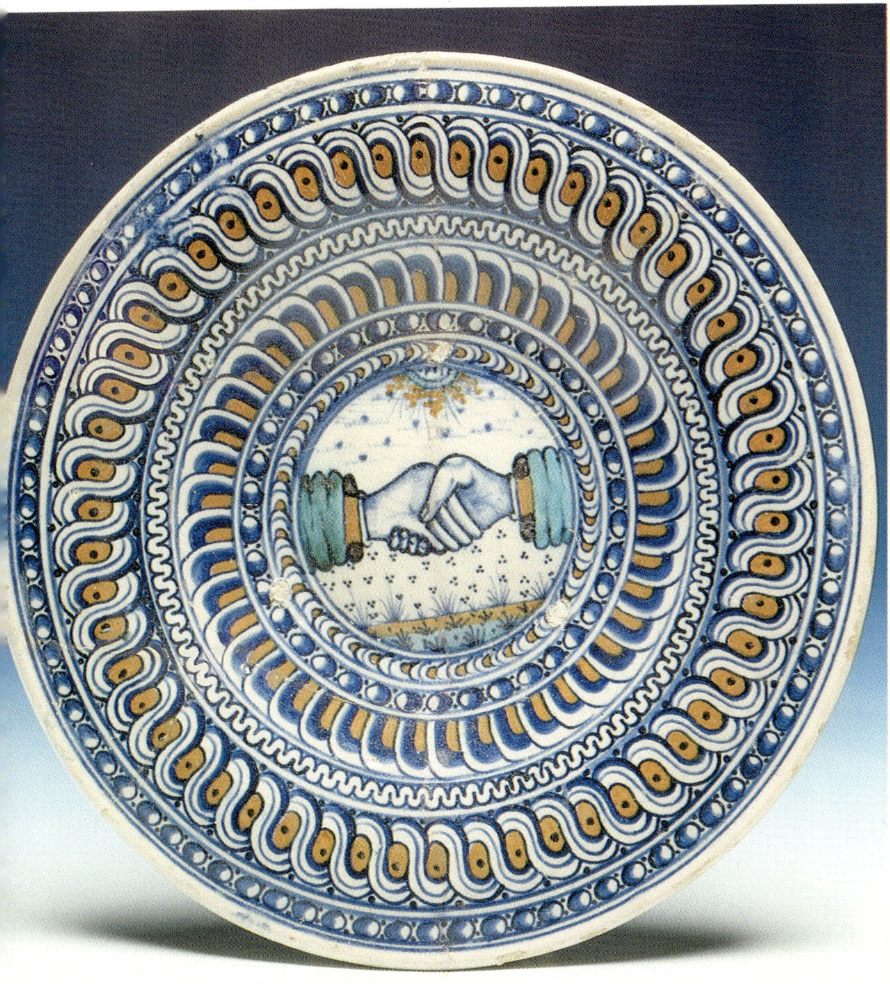

Cafaggiolo

Supported by the dei Medici family of Florence and set up on the ruins of a pre-existent brick furnace, a centre for the production of majolica was built up which reached such a degree of perfection as to be able to satisfy all the requirements of the dei Medici family.

This great success is largely due to the Fattorini fami-

INK STAND. Faenza, sixteenth century. Multi-coloured ink stand in the form of the nativity scene. The pen holder supported by three lions bears the inscription on the base "verbum charo fatum est de vergine maria".

ly, who moved from Montelupo to Cafaggiolo on the invitation of Lorenzo de' Medici. And it was here that for three centuries the Fattorinis took charge of production for the dei Medici family.

The majolica of Montelupo had a vital influence on that of Cafaggiolo, although later a disctintive style emerged in terms of design and the use of a range of colour tones. The backgrounds are mainly a lively deep sky blue roughly and heavily applied with the brush. The green is clear and transparent and there is frequent use of an unusual cherry red and lemon yellow. A few examples of majolica from Cafaggiolo bear a trident summounted with the initials "SPR" or "SPF". Others only show the letter"P" or "PF".

A great many large ceramic products conserved in various museums were manufactured in Cafaggiolo.

Siena

In this Tuscan city a large amount of ancient style pottery was already produced in 1265. It seems that tall jugs with splayed legs and decorated with animal and vegetal motifs were the most widely made kind of object.

The production of majolica in this city began in 1510 and continued throughout the sixteenth century. But unfortunately only very few works from this "good period" have come down to us. Sienese majolica is often mistaken for that of Cafaggiolo because of the similar kind of paste used and the similarity of the decorations.

In Kensington Museum there is a splendid display plate with the figure of Saint Jerome beautifully painted on it and bearing the words "made in Siena by Master Benedict".

It is therefore possible to connect a production of beautifully worked majolica in terms of decoration and design with the school of Master Benedict who was ac-

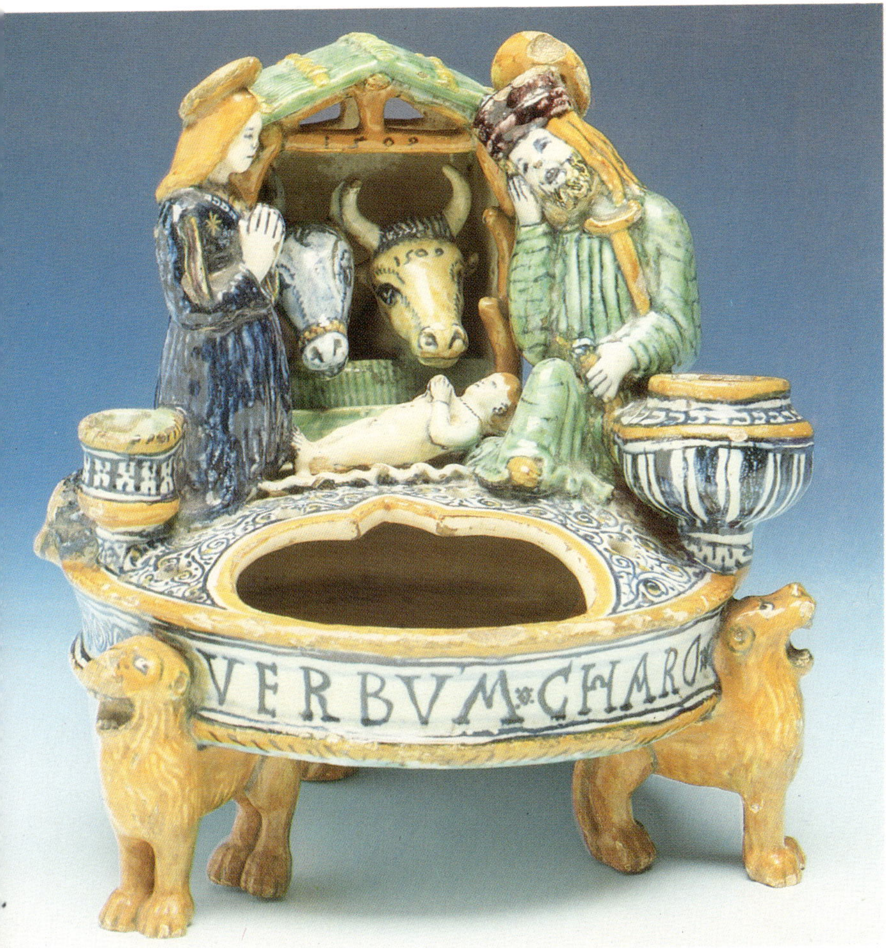

tive in Siena in the sixteenth century. In such work the main subjects (saints and mythological figures) are bordered by the arabesques typical of the ancient pottery.

A great many works of majolica produced in Siena in the sixteenth century are anonymous, despite their incomparable beauty and distinctiveness of pictorial style. For this reason they are usually defined "Master of Saint Sebastian plate" (Victoria and Albert Museum),

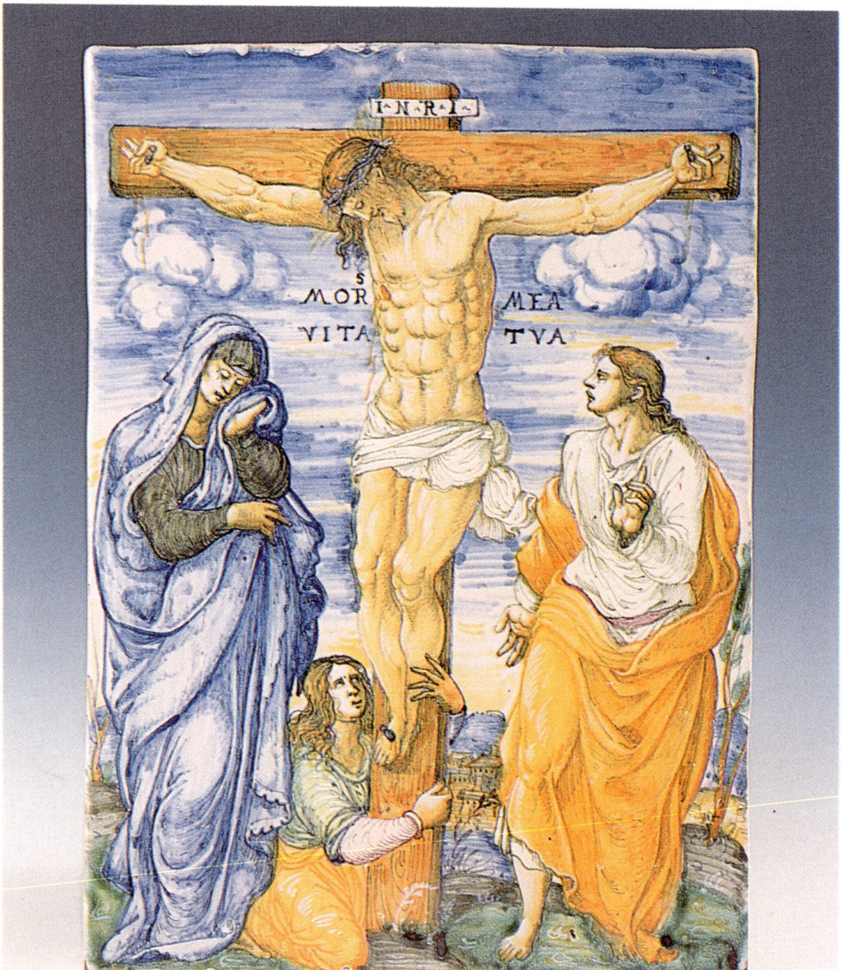

"Master of Saint John", "Master of the Resurrection" or "Master of the Assumption" and so on.

Emilia-Romagnia - Faenza

Faenza is the glory of Italy, writes De Mauri in his book "L'amatore di maiolica e porcellane" (The lover of Majolica and Porcelain), not because it was the first place in which majolica was made, but because of the high quality of the craftsmanship in producing works covered in tin-based paint and because this opened up the commerce of Italian ceramics to the whole of Europe. Indeed, still today the term "Faince" is used to describe a kind of product made of a soft, dull and slightly coloured clay, and coated with paint which has been given a mat finish by the addition of tin powder.

The pottery manufactured in Faenza until the end of the 1500s is certainly not inferior to that produced in other centres in Italy. Indeed, the majolica produced between 1500 and 1530 can be considered among the best in the whole of the peninsular, including Cafaggiolo.

Among the examples from the late 1400s and early 1500s there are plaques, tiles, chemist's vases, spherical jugs with handles in the shape of winged dragons, chemist's recepticles with spouts in the shape of serpents, and large plates and trays.

These products are distinctive in their lively and bright colours, especially the blue, the wonderful design of their figures and their perfect proportion of form. Typical features of the work from Faenza are the tasteful use of Renaissance decorative motifs. Influenced by the work of the nearby Della Robbia family, the end of the 1400s in Faenza saw the rise of a new genre in ceramics made up of plaques and and bas-relief panels.

At the beginning of the sixteenth century we find the first examples of the so-called "berettino" (little cap), one of the most commonly used types of decoration in Faenza, characterized by slate-blue paint with mat white decorations. Worthy of note are a few plates which have a putto or coat of arms in the hollow of the plate and a wide decorated border in which the harmony of colours is still based around the use of blue and

RECTANGULAR PLAQUE.
Pesaro, middle of the sixteenth century.
Multi-coloured majolica plaque showing the crucifixion.
At the centre Christ with his head reclining on his right shoulder.
At his side and feet, Saint John and Mary Magdalen.
By the sides of the cross the words "mors mea vita tua".

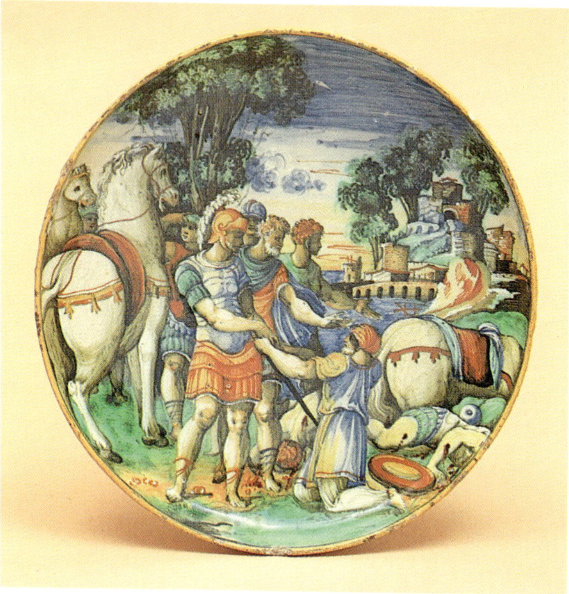

HISTORICAL DESIGN FRUIT STAND. Urbino, 1545. Multi-coloured majolica showing a mythological scene in blue, copper green, ochre and yellow with figures and landscape background. Low circular base.

white.

The very elaborate and expertly painted "grotesque" decorations, which belong to the best period of production in Faenza may be attributed to any one of about eight important artists, among whom are Zoan Maria Vasaro and Niccolò Pellipario.

Around 1570 a new and original style of decorative painting was introduced called "compendiario" (brief), so-called because of the way it was carried out in short, brief sketches, often in one colour, a splash of washed blue, of yellow, of green, painted onto the rough and white glaze, from which we get the name "Bianchi" (Whites) used to describe this type of rather beautiful majolica.

Pesaro

In Pesaro, near Urbino, the production of ancient pottery decorated with coats of arms, stylized animal and vegetal forms or geometric patterns "scratched" onto jugs, bowls and dishes, is not very different from the other work produced in central Italy.

Luca della Robbia's technique of glazing and colouring terracotta reached Pesaro towards 1470 and soon spread to and influenced production at the centres of Urbino and Casteldurante.

In 1500 the rule of the Sforzas came to an end and power passed to the Della Rovere family, the Dukes of Urbino and rulers of Pesaro. Under their government the arts flourished, including the manufacture of majolica which reached great heights with the splendid "Istriati" (history) pieces which were decorated with historical scenes.

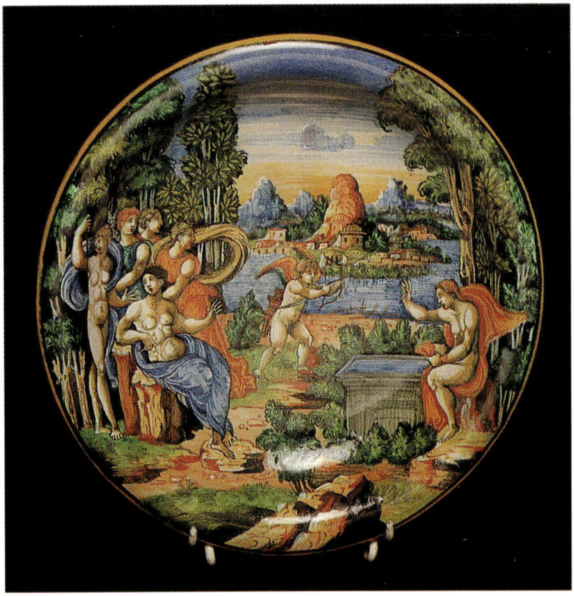

HISTORICAL DESIGN PLATE. Urbino, sixteenth century. Multi-coloured decoration showing the myth of Narcissus and Echo. On the back, in the ring of the base, the inscription "il l'uomo amante di sua imago" and the date 1546. Workshop of Xanto Avelli of Urbino.

Pesaro, then, had a large number of majolica craftsmen and painters who excelled in this historical style. Here we give only a few of those who were active in the city in the sixteenth century: Girolamo Lanfranco delle Gabicce and his son Giacomo, who produced some fine examples between 1540 and 1542, the Masters Bernardino Gagliardino, Baldassarre the potter of Pesaro and Terentino, son of master majolica craftsman Matteo.

Sacred, mythological and profane stories, painted on plates and vases by Orazio Fontana, Franco Veneziano and Raffaele del Borgo, dominate majolica production in this period. The colours are extremely beautiful and are used in such a way that they preserve their transparency, rendered all the more delicate by the light paste beneath. The motifs of groups, arabesques, trophies, fruits and trees were wonderfully depicted. The handles and grotesque masks of the vases were unusual and beautifully crafted.

Urbino

Urbino was an important ceramics centre in the sixteenth century. Together with Casteldurante and Gubbio this city was governed by the Duke of Urbino.

MODELLED FIGURE. Urbino, end of the 1500s. Terracotta majolica showing mother and child. At the feet of the Madonna, Saint John offering a dove and a cat. On the three sides of the base, on a white background, a "grotesque" decorative motif. Characteristic range of colour tones in the yellow, orange, blue, green and black. From the Patanazzi workshop.

Although there had been kilns here right from 1477, the production of majolica, for which Urbino would become famous the world over, only achieved high artistic standards after 1520 - 30. Nevertheless it must be stated that in 1491 a few master potters made a particularly beautiful majolica floor for the Bishop of Padova Pietro Barozzi.

In the first half, or more precisely in the first 25 years, of the sixteenth century, ceramics production at Urbino proceeded at the same pace as at Casteldurante and Gubbio. But when Guido Pellipario, son of Niccolò, set himself up in Urbino, then a new creative spirit was breathed into majolica manufacturing and the city began to producce work in a new and grandious style. When Guido Pellipario set up his workshop in Urbino he took the name of the Fontana family. The majolica he and his son Orazio Fontana produced was immediately distinguished by the deep artistic culture which it displayed in the compositions inspired by works by Raffaello and in the use of metallic yellow and ruby red. This majolica belongs to the best period of production in Urbino.

And yet the greatest name in majolica in Urbino is Francesco Xanto Avelli da Rovigo. Although he was influenced by Niccolò Pellipario, his work is distinctive for its peculiar vivacity and density of colour as well as for its great compositional sensitivity. Differently from Pellipario, who created designs which were adapted to the plates, Francesco Xanto Avelli filled the empty spaces of the composition with figures taken from engravings of the period.

His works are signed with the initials "F.X.A.R" and with various combinations or simplifications of these. Around the work of Francesco Avelli there developed the work of descendents of Pellipario and the Fontanas. This was characterized by the use of warm colours, especially yellow, and by the masterly use of design.

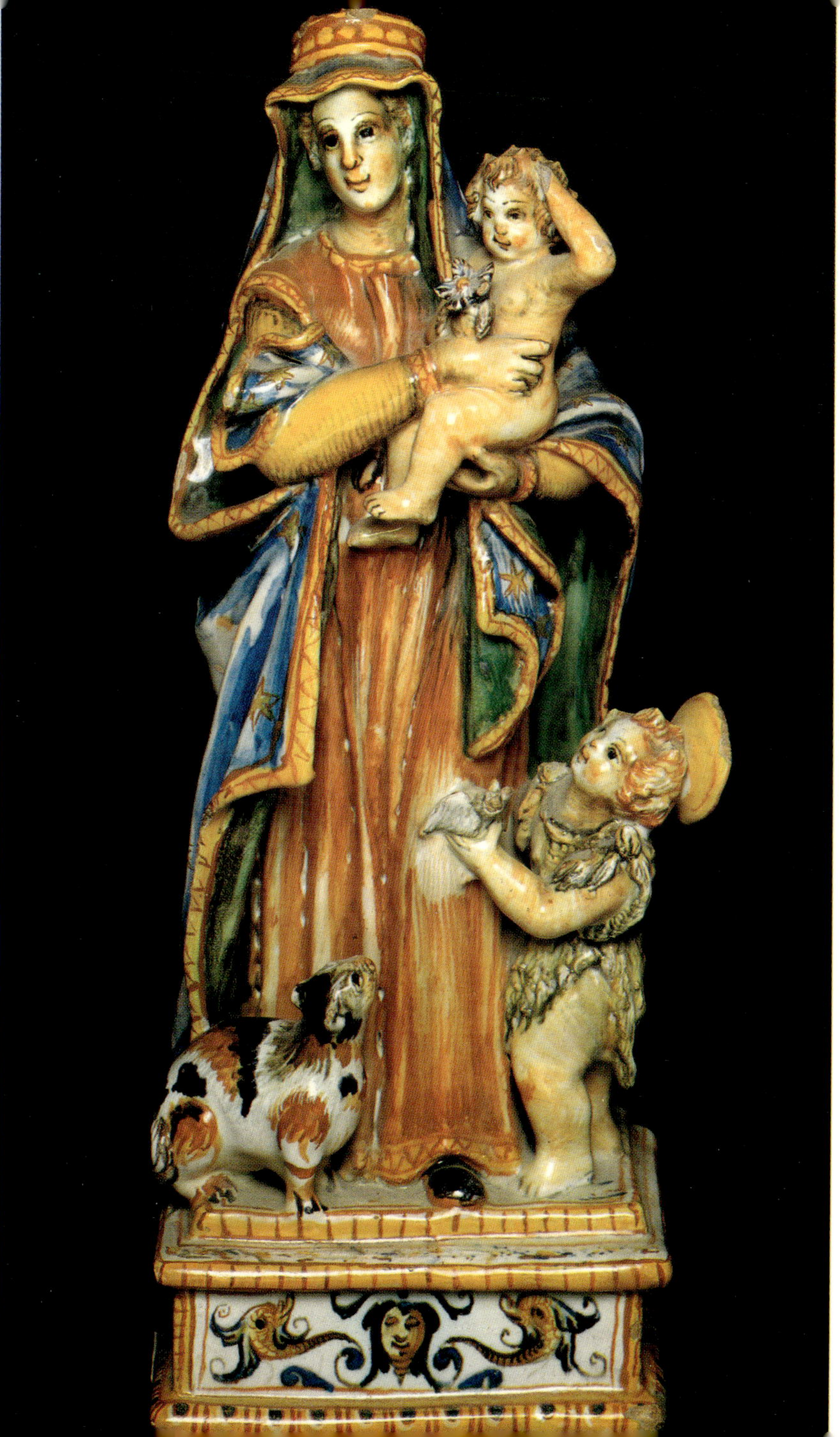

PUCKERED PLATE. Casteldurante, sixteenth century. Puckered majolica plate with four-part multi-coloured decoration. In the centre a "trophy" motif enclosed within radial sections painted in alternate decorative motifs. Along the edge a strip of leaves.

Towards 1570 there began to appear an extremely delicate "grotesque" decoration known as "Raphaelesque" which eventually replaced the taste for the "historical" style.

The grotesques were frequently applied to works having handles in the shape of dolphins, round figures, masks and other plastic motifs. This type of decoration appeared on majolica produced in Urbino until the middle of the 1600s. We have no knowledge of later production.

Casteldurante

Casteldurante is the present day Urbania, a small town not very far from Urbino, which changed its name in 1636 in honour of Pope Urbane VIII.

Here we find the "Beauty" style, which has its origin in Faenza, in combination with high quality majolica produced from the clay of the river Metauro.

Production at Casteldurante in the 1500s owes much to the potter Zoan Maria who had a decisive influence on decorative styles. This master majolica craftsman created a goblet for Pope Julius II in 1508 which immediately became famous. The entire object is covered with bizarre putti, sphinxes, candlesticks, flowers, leaves and arms which alternate symmetrically on a dark background, thus producing a harmonious pattern of the most diverse and varied motifs. Pope Julius's goblet is housed in the Metropolitan Museum in New York and is much admired by ceramics collectors.

Side developments of the "Casteldurante Historical" genre were: the "white on white" style, loving cups and busts of helmeted warriers. The loving cup usually has the portrait of a woman covering the whole surface, the image of the face standing out against the dark blue background of the concave surface, while a fluttering ribbon bears her name. These cups, like the "Beauty"

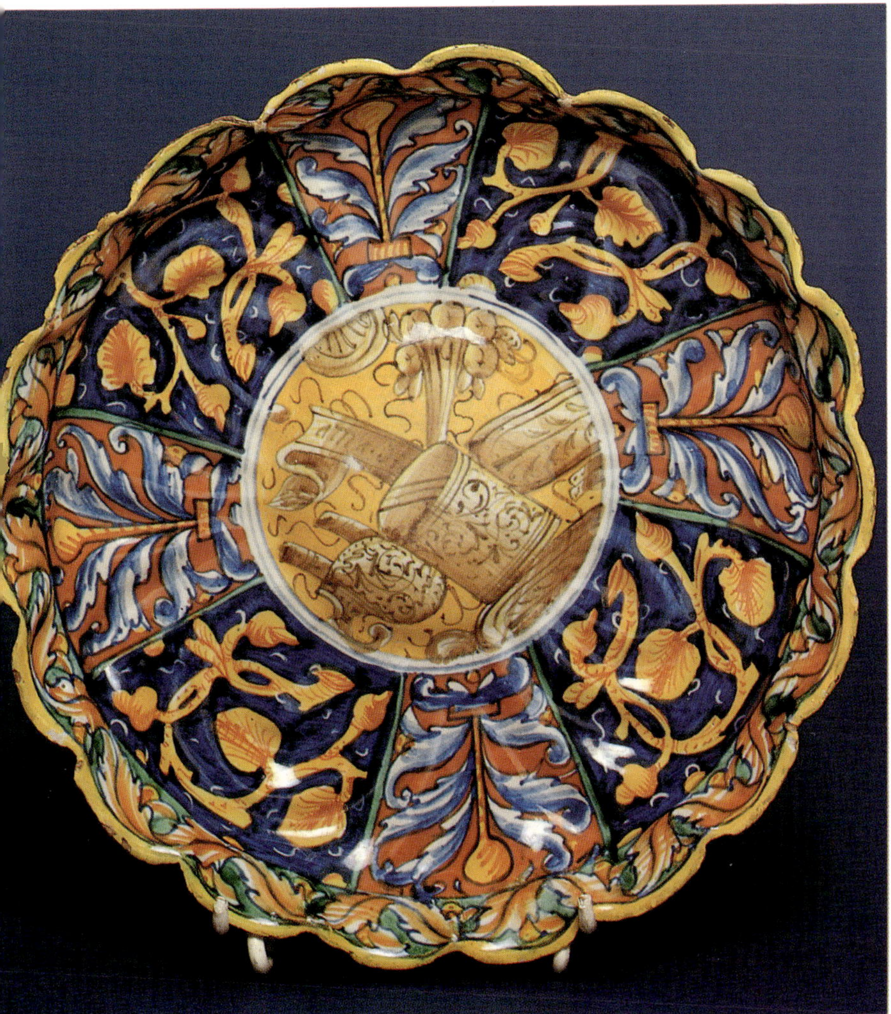

plates, were usually given on an engagement as a pledge of love.

It is right to maintain that some of the "metallic gloss" ceramics were sent to Gubbio to be enriched with irridescent reflections created by the celebrated Master Giorgio, who took his secret technique with him to the grave.

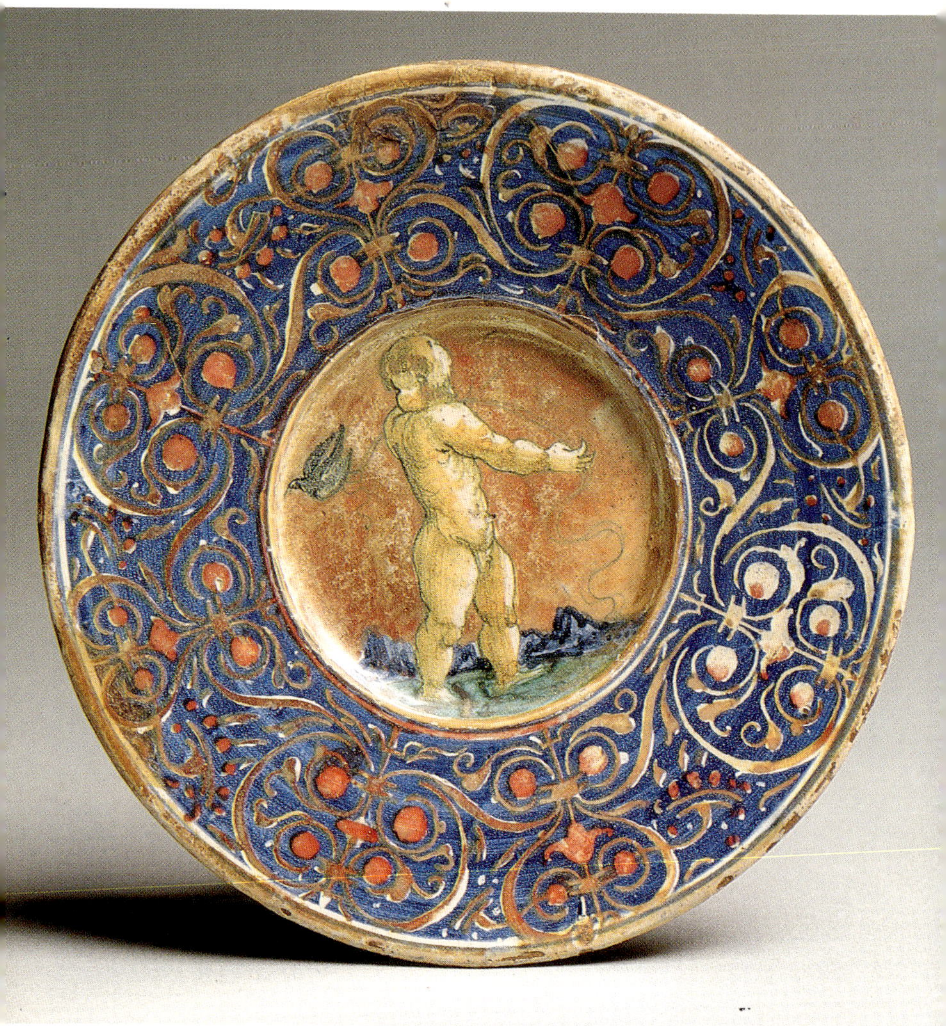

Liguria and the centres of Genoa, Savona and Albisola

In the Renaissance there were three important centres for the production of majolica: Genoa, Savona and nearby Albisola. The importance of maritime trade to these places led in the 1500s to the production of a distinctive Ligurian genre of ceramics characterized by tiles of Arab origin (called "zullagium" in Arabic) for floors or walls, monochrome products or decorations with multi-coloured geometrical designs. There are many examples of walls covered with these tiles which can still be admired in a great many Genoese and Savonese palaces.

The Ligurian majolica craftsmen of the 1500s perfected this unusual technique to such an extent that they were able to use these "zullagium" tiles in splendid compositions forming part of huge mosaics in both church and civil buildings alike: Saint John the Baptist and Saint George, the Genoese church of Santa Maria di Castello, the majolica panel depicting Marcello the warrier and other characters, which is now preserved in Turin on the first floor of the Madama building, and which originally comes from the hall of the Pavesi Palace in Savona, the adoration of the shepherds in the parish church of "nostra Signora della Concordia" in Albisola.

The practice of covering walls with painted tiles goes back to ancient times. Already three thousand years before Christ the tomb of Pharaoh Zoser was covered with green tiles with yellow parts in relief. In the sixth century BC the door of ISHTAR which led into the holy way (in Babylon) was sparkling with the light blue of the painted tiles showing bulls and two-headed dragons. This practice came to Liguria from the Near East through Spain around 1250. The earliest examples were almost certainly imported artifacts, but later on they were also produced independently in Savona. The first motifs were based on Islamic designs involving interwoven geometrical patterns. The usual colours were green, light blue, black and yellow. In the second half of the fifteenth century we begin to see the first heraldic coats of arms appearing on

GLOSSY PLATE. Gubbio, 1520-30. Glossy plate in golden yellow and ruby red, decorated in the centre with a putto and bird on a mountanous background. Along the border a spiral decoration and berries on deep blue background.

CEREMONIAL PLATE. Deruta, 1525. Glossy plate in golden yellow and decorated in blue. At the centre a young girl with long hair and jewels plays the viola. The border is decorated with "tile" panels which alternate with swirling foliage.

Ligurian tiles, while in the 1500s the decorations are generally figurative mosaic compositions based on Renaissance models.

Besides painted tiles, the 1500s in Liguria also saw the the production of a great amount of pottery (in Ligurian ports a great variety of Oriental products could be found - materials, carpets, bronzes and naturally also ceramics). For this reason a clear Oriental influence can be detected on the Ligurian majolica of the period, not only in the scroll decorations or natural flowing lines carried out in blue on a pale blue background, but also in the arabesques, vegetal motifs that form a complicated rose pattern in the centre of the piece with an unusual heart- shaped border all around.

Gubbio

Collectors all over the world admire sixteenth century majolica produced in Gubbio, which in those times formed part of the Dukedom of Urbino, mainly because of the rare and extraordinary beauty of the glossy metallic decorations and their peculiar changing tones of red. The shape of the majolica derives from designs produced by Master Giorgio, and the figures and decorations are not very original and in any case are very similar to those of Deruta and other ceramics centres.

As a result Gubbio's fame for ceramics in the sixteenth century is inevitably bound up with the famous majolica polisher Master Giorgio. A native of Intra, he settled with his family in the early 1500s in quarter of Saint Andrea, hence the method of siging his precious pieces "mastro giorgio da ugubio" - Master Giorgio of Gubbio. Nevertheless he adopted numerous other signatures and initials accompanied by the date of production: M.G. 1515 (the oldest which we know about), G.A. dangubio 1520 (the A. stands for Andreoli, his

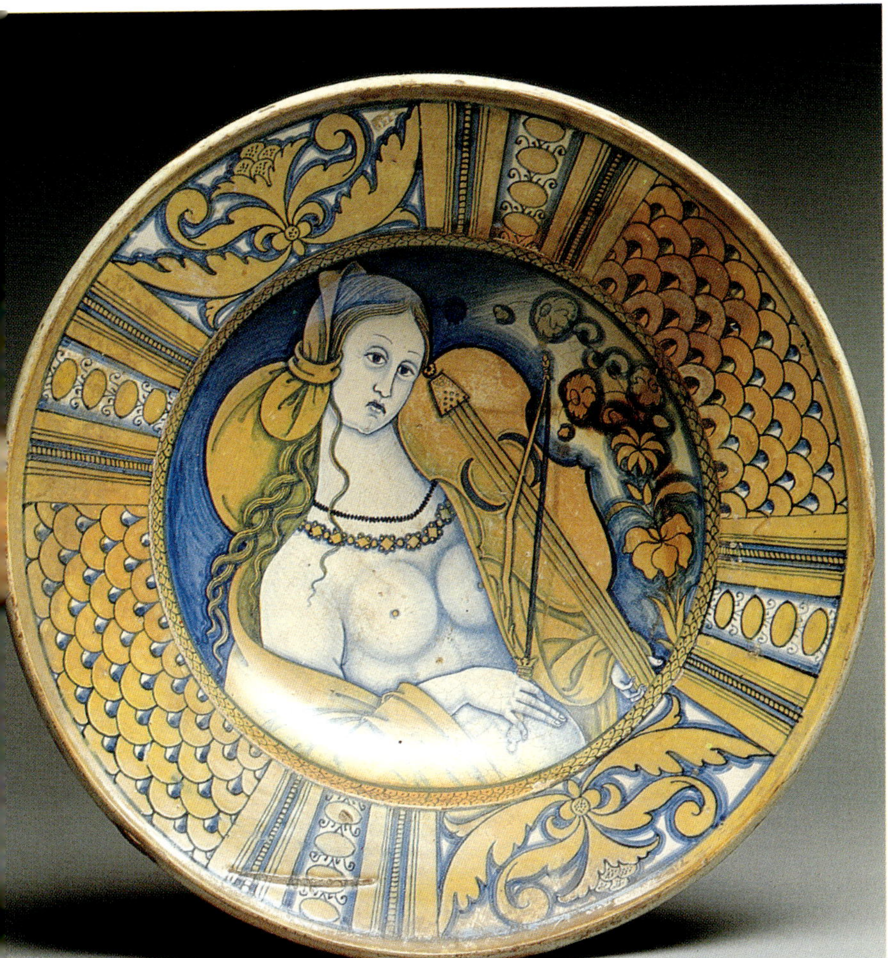

surname) a.G 1522, Ungubio mastro Girgio 1528 and many others.

Master Giorgio died around the year 1553, taking with him to the grave a few precious secrets concerning a particular polishing technique which he did not want anybody to know about, not even his brother Ubaldo, who was a polisher in Andreoli's own work-

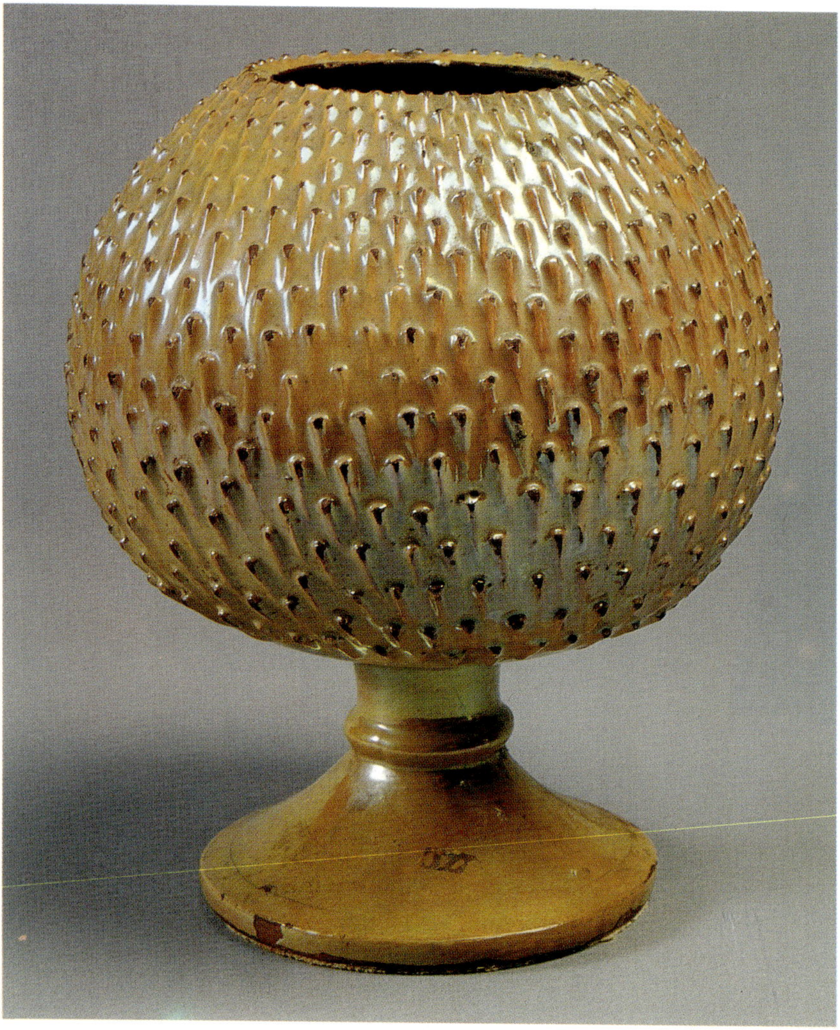

shop, or his son Vincenzo, known as "the Rag", to whom Master Giorgio entrusted his affairs in 1536.

It is by now well known that besides the works carried out by himself and his flourishing workshop, Master Giorgio also achieved irridiscent reflections by means of a third firing on pieces made by other artists not only in Gubbio but also in the neighbouring areas.

CONE-SHAPEDVASE. Deruta, circa 1525. Cone-shaped vase in glossy golden yellow. Short stem with ring in relief. Tapering circular base.

Venice

Glazed terracotta had been produced in Venice right from the twelvth and thirteenth centuries, but the first examples of majolica appear in the city only around 1510. These are few plates with a rather transparent glaze due to the small amount of tin oxide used. The most common staniferous gloss paint which appears on Venetian majolica has an extremely pale blue background, often tending towards grey, called "smaltino".

The decorations are known as "porcelain" style and derive from Chinese motifs, specifically of the Ming period. Otherwise the decorations are in plain light blue with interwoven oak branches. A few plates of particularly fine craftsmanship bear the arms of alliance of certain German families, testifying to the close commercial ties between parts of Germany and Venice.

Because of Venice's many relations with the Orient, some works reflect the influence of that civilization. Thus we find lotus flower decorations and Chinese style fluttering foliage. One variety of sixteenth century majolica is in the "historical" stlye of Urbino, but with colours which are too strong for the delicacy of the design. Another presents festoons of flowers and leaves painted in strong colours against a pale blue background with panels portraying heads, busts and complete figures. Besides the pieces already described there are also a fair number having the characteristic deep blue background decorated with architectural views, stylized vine leaves, fruit and rose patterns in vivid colours which appear to have been influenced by contemporary Venetian painting.

In Padova too, around the middle of the sixteenth century, we find some beautiful majolica with "historical" designs bearing the name of the city and date on the back. But this work is strongly influenced by nearby Venice.

DERUDA MAJOLICA PIECE. Sixteenth century. Deruta stoup from the middle of the 1500s. This unusual piece which was for domestic use was placed beside the bed. Multi-coloured decorations with "Raphaelesque" motifs. Two small spiral columns frame the central part in which we can see the archangel leading Tobit. In the upper part two winged putti; in the lower part a modelled basin to contain the holy water, decorated with a noble coat of arms.

Deruta

Deruta is a small town situated on the river Tiber between Perugia and Todi, and it is from here that we get some of the finest examples of sixteenth century majolica painted with a glossy metallic finish.

At the end of the 1400s majolica was produced here of a particularly high artistic standard, due largely to the presence of the artistic school which provided designs taken from the work of Perugino and Pinturicchio.

The work produced in the sixteenth century attempts to achieve fine surfaces and rare effects of light and colour. One of the most important kinds of work produced in Deruta is the so- called reverse-leaf style, in which the back of the piece is also decorated with vegetal motifs. Also worthy of note are the pieces decorated in tawny, changing tones, in gold and mother-of- pearl over polychrome gloss, a techique of Moorish origin, like the metallic gloss finish. (The famous glossy-metallic reflections of rare beauty are in tones of gold, mother-o-pearl and ruby red).

The palette used by the potters of Deruta was incomparably rich in different pigments ranging from blue to orange and from yellow to green with the addition at the third firing of the final coating of metallic gloss. The best majolica of this type was carried out before 1530.

Busts, figures and both sacred and profane scenes are painted in the centre of large plates with wide edges, as well as on the characteristic pot-bellied jugs and slender stemmed goblets.

Also produced in large quantities at Deruta were modelled figures, bas-reliefs, votive plaques and paving tiles. The potters of Deruta hardly ever signed their work. The initials which may be found on the back are not identifiable and in any case appear to refer to the purchaser rather than the maker. One exception is a monk of Deruta, the maker of a few display plates with

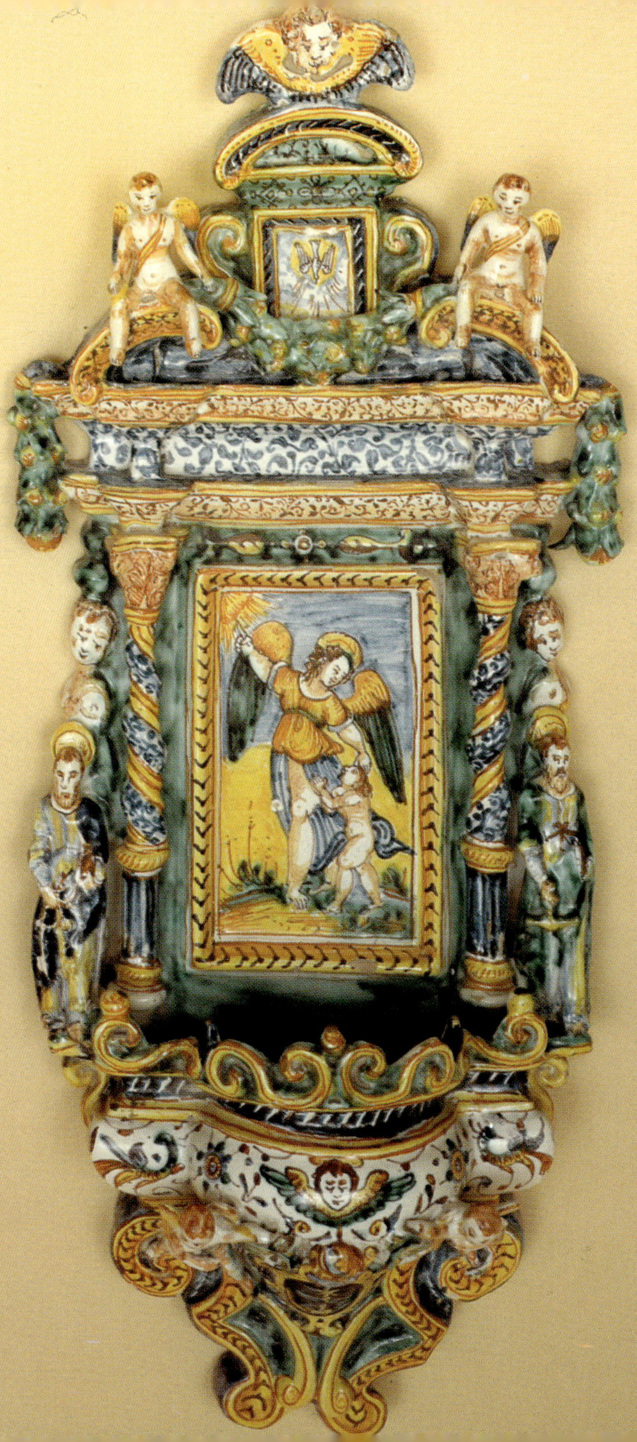

DISPLAY PLATE. Deruta, 1500s. Plate with multi-coloured decoration with central medallion showing the "Holy family". Wide border decorated with "Persian palm" motifs alternating with rose patterns and enclosed within two geometrically patterned concentric bands.

historical decorations taken from an edition of "Orlando Furioso". This monk's works are dated between 1541 and 1545.

The most important work produced in Deruta in the 1500s is without doubt the floor of the church of Saint Francis in Deruta, dated 1524. The tiles are laid in a mosaic to form figures with allegories of the virtues, the muses, sybils and Helios on the chariot of the sun. All around there are festoons which border the scenes. The artist is anonymous, and is known simply as the "master of the floor".

Naples

The majolica produced in the region of Campania in the sixteenth century represented all the various kinds of ceramic artifact known in those times. Unfortunately, however, these works are poorly documented except for a few wall and floor decorations which are still preserved in public and church buildings, signed by the craftsmen who carried out the work, such as Nardo Rao, whose name can be seen on the floor of the Church of the Annunciation, or else Pietro of Aversa, the craftsman responsible for the floor which at one time could be found in the Ducal Palace of Palma.

A few ceramic workers in Campania are documented elsewhere in Italy, such as Master Bernardino de Gentili in Tivoli, and Giovanni Maria Da Capua, who is documented as far away as Belgium. All this testifies to the high quality of Neapolitan majolica ware produced in the sixteenth century, and as a result its export to various other regionsd and countries.

The shapes of Neapolitan floor tiles were rather unusual. They were created in groups and each nucleus was composed of tiles in tapezoid, hexagonal, square or rectangular forms. When put together according to some pre-conceived design, they produced a "figurative deco-

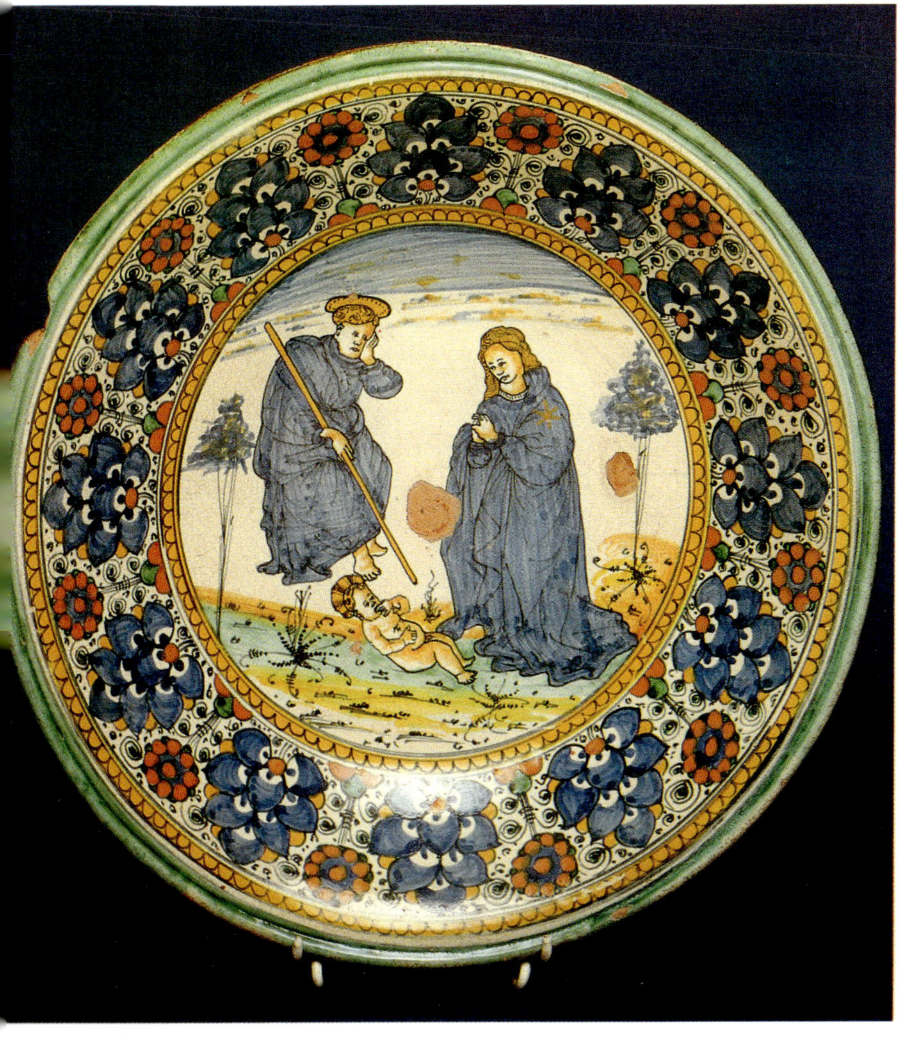

rative" mosaic which was both beautiful and lively, composed of deep tones of yellow, orange and deep blue.

Castelli d'Abruzzo

Until a short time ago the fame of this ceramics centre was tied to the work produced in the seventeenth

FOUR «ZULLAGIUM» TILES. Savona, sixteenth century. Four "zullagium" tiles forming a single design of Hispanic-Moorish origin. White majolica from Savona with multi-coloured decoration: blue, white, green and yellow. The production of painted tiles to cover the walls and floors of religious buildings and create artistic flooring is a Ligurian tradition in ceramics that dates back to the thirteenth century.

and eighteenth centuries. Indeed, sixteenth century work was practically unknown, consisting of a few examples of glazed floor tiles now preserved in the local museum, and ceramic ware for chemists' shops such as jugs with spouts, pots and vases.

However, recent excavations begun in 1980 on the slopes of Gran Sasso a few metres away from a glacier, have brought to light some extraordinary examples and many fragments which indicate the existence of high quality majolica ware that developed in Castelli through the work of the Pompei family.

During the excavations some extraordinary finds have been unearthed all of which demonstate the great variety and beauty of the majolica produced by this great family of majolica craftsmen. As a result, many pieces from Castelli d'Abruzzo have found their way into museums and private collections: unusual blue sauce boats with white decorations, double-handled vases with beautifully worked profiles of young women, jugs with dragon-headed spouts, plates in deep blue produced for the higher ranks of society. In the second half of the sixteenth century, Castelli also produced rather well-made ordinary crockery.

As is understandable, then, the history of ceramics is in continual evolution. The example of the excavations at Castelli are clear evidence of this. Every year new publications are added to the hundreds already available in Italy, providing greater knowledge of majolica and ceramics in general.

Palermo

As a flourishing port, busy with trade of every type, Palermo in the sixteenth century was an important centre for the import and export of all kinds of ceramics.

Consequently the local production of majolica, which was flourishing then, was influenced both by Oriental

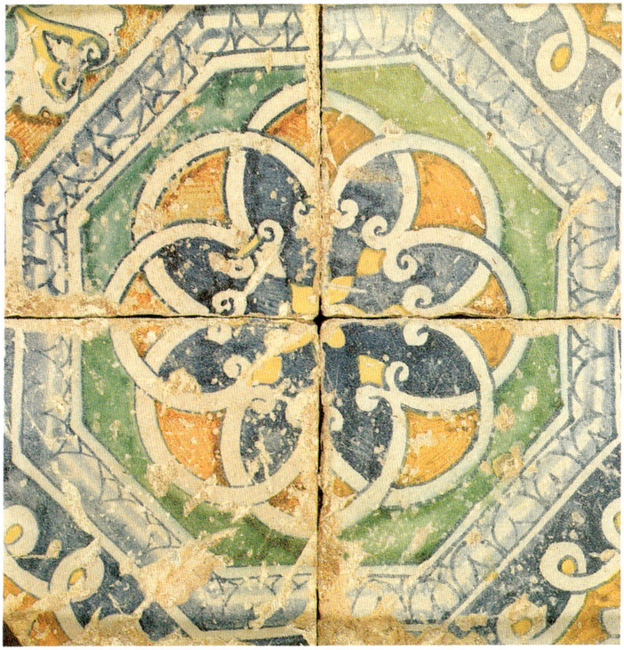

methods of ceramic decoration as well as that of other maritime cities such as Venice, Genoa and Naples.

The work produced in Palermo, especially concerning chemist's equipment, is mainly distinguished by its lively colours and so-called "Floral" style with festoons, wreaths of leaves, trophies and decorative motifs inspired by Ancient Greece, each pattern neatly and clearly divided from the other. The animal and sometimes human figures which are often found in the centre of these decorations, are simply done, without any pretence to sharpness of line or elegance of design. These ways of working went on until the late seventeenth century.

Caltagirone

This is certainly the most ancient and famous centre of ceramics in the whole of Sicily. Like other parts of the island in the fourteenth and fifteenth centuries,

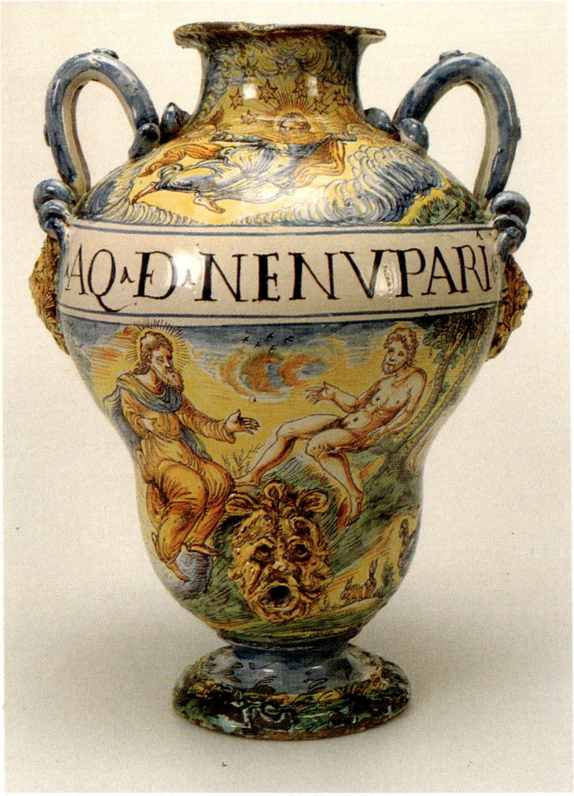

Pair of large chemist's vases. Savona, end of the sixteenth century. Pair of large chemist's vases in Savona majolica made in the late sixteenth century. These "baluster" vases, also called hydrias were used for containing curative waters. Indeed, the inscriptions on the scroll reads "aq.d.nenupari" and "aq.pulegy". The two hydrias are decorated with biblical scenes taken from the Old Testament and are wonderfully painted in harmonious tones of yellow, green and blue.

Caltagirone came under a Spanish-Catalan-Arabic influence. But with the beginning of the 1500s a style which can be defined Renaissaince-Siculan began to assert itself. This happened because of the massive importation of majolica from the Tuscan centres of Montelupo and Siena as well as those in the Marches such as Casteldurante and Urbino, brought there by Tuscan merchants who roamed all over the Mediterranean with their goods.

Castigiorone may be considered the most important centre in Sicily in terms of the amount of majolica produced. But the work is inspired largely by models coming from elsewhere in Italy, and is therefore without great originality. Nevertheless, they are distinguished

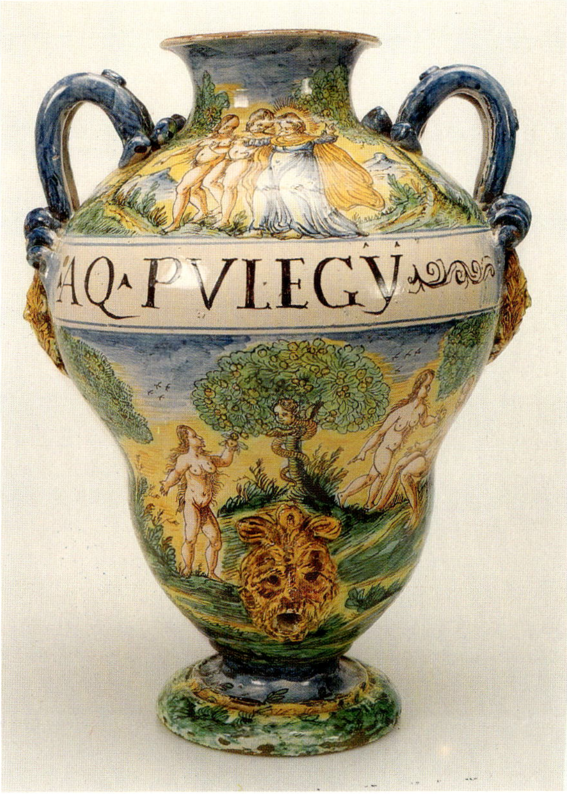

by the use of a wide range of intense and lively colours, undoubtedly due to the warmth and sun which brightens even the dullest tones.

Characteristic and unusual, on the other hand, are the products made in Caltagirone towards the end of the sixteenth century and throughout the whole of the 1600s. In the eighteenth century we find terracotta figures of shepherds, peasants people at work and contemporary Sicilian characters. Besides being original works, they are also particularly attractive.

The good season of the 17th and 18th century Italian manufacturing

Faenza

The Urbino school of the end of the 1500s, which was overflowing with decorations that completely covered the artifact, signalled the high point of the historical and grotesque style of ceramics. The beautiful Renaissance period and "way of doing ceramics" was therefore about to end and give way to the "COMPENDIARIO" or "brief" style of Faenza. This began around

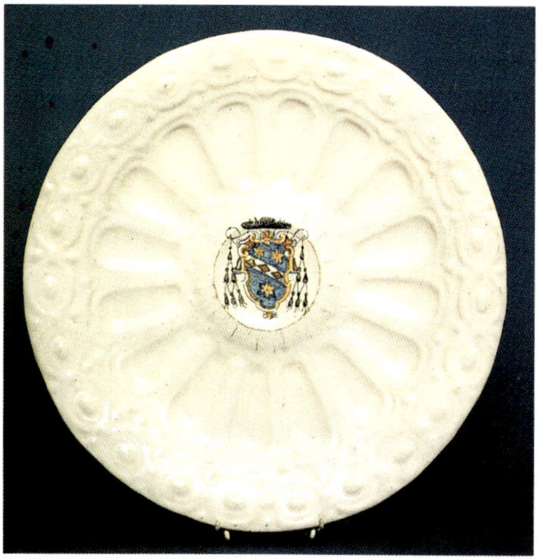

1570 and was characterized by quick workmanship with the decorations sketched roughly in a single colour such as pale blue, pale yellow or pale green painted onto a rough and white glaze. Hence this unusual and simple kind of majolica has been given the name "white of Faenza".

FAENZA PLATE. Seventeenth century. The "brief" style of Faenza. The centre bears the emblem of a cardinal.

MULTI-COLOURED PLATE. Seventeenth century Savona plate with multi-coloured decorations showing the theme of the hero who fights the monster and saves the young girl Andromeda.

This style was the most suited to bring out the emerging baroque forms which were being applied to ceramics and were taken mainly from the silverware of the period: large, modelled trays, display plates, drink coolers and other objects.

It was the craftsmen of Faenza, then, who first understood that the glorious Renaissance period had come to an end and who therefore gave life to a new way of working which would develop throughout the seventeenth century into the most magnificent and unusual motifs and decorations.

The greatest exponents of the "brief" style were Virgiliotto Calamelli and Leonardo Bettisti known as "Don Pino".

The eighteenth century in Faenza is dominated by the famous Fermiani factory, which produced some of the best ceramics in Faenza in the 1700s and a good portion of the 1800s too.

The factory was founded in 1693 by Count Annibale Ferniani and it stayed in production until 1893. Still today the shapes and decorations of this famous ceramic ware are widely reproduced on plates, saucers, cups, soup dishes and vases by producers both in Faenza and elsewhere.

The factory began producing majolica in 1768 with

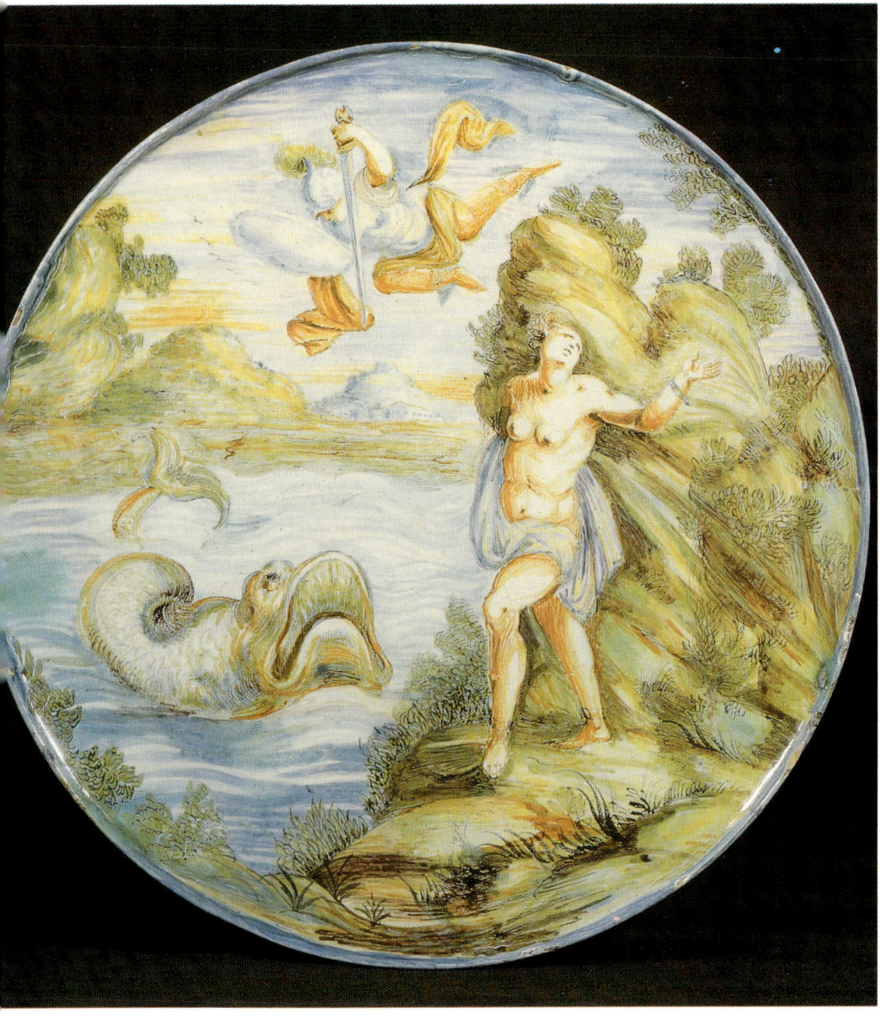

Count Annibale the second, a man of great culture who made several visits to the far east in order to study the techniques and decorations in use there, bringing up to date his own manufacture to suit the new taste for Chinese and Oriental designs.

In 1773, the third firing technique was used for the

BALUSTERVASE. Savona, seventeenth century. Typical baluster vase in pale blue majolica with the "arms of Savona". The handles are in the form of serpents coiled at the ends. The decoration in cobalt blue is typical of Ligurian majolica of the 1600s with putti, ruins, farmhouses, travellers and mountainous backgrounds.

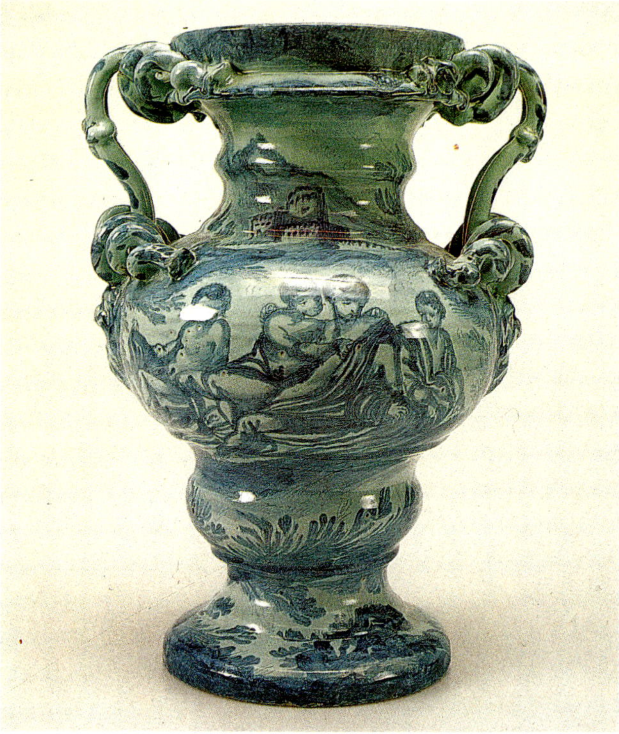

first time in this workshop. This technique was able to produce lively and varied colours which it had never before been possible to create. The most famous decorations coming from the Ferniani factory are the "carnation" the "little villages", "small figures", "the hut" and the "bunches of flowers", all of which are carried out in varied colours or else in green and brown known as "comerio".

The Majolica of Savona

In the baroque age the art of making and decorating ceramics belongs to Savona-Albisola, where enormous amounts of majolica were produced right from the beginning of the seventeenth century. Characteristic of these pieces were the unusual embellishments on the decorations and the use of the deep blue colour.

The rich and prosperous Genoa of the 1600s, which previously had seen the rise of a few local ceramics factories, tended to abandon this product in favour of silverware, which was more suited to the luxurious furnishings of the Genoese patrician palaces.

The once prolific production in Savona later received a further creative impetus inspired by contemporary Ligurian painting. The new style was well suited to the shapes of baroque pods, display plates and modelled vases decorated with quick sketches of saints, nymphs and putti in a pictorial synthesis worthy of many contemporary artists. It is exactly this liveliness of craftsmanship that makes Ligurian majolica of the 1600s so unusual and striking. It was a way of working that would be a source of inspiration for many other ceramics decorators, particularly in France.

In the seventeenth and eighteenth centuries ceramics decoration in Savona takes on its own artistic shape and the style became an important feature of the baroque period in Italy as a whole. Among the many artists working in the field, the Guidobono family particularly stand out. The head of the family, Giovani Antonio (1631-1685), who first perfected the chiaroscuro of plain deep blue, and his son Bartolomeo, called the painter and majolica decorator priest of

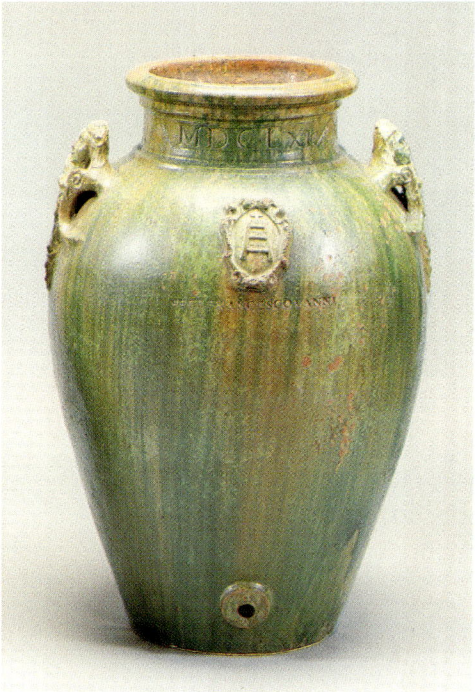

Jug.
Siena, ceventeenth century.
Large jug sponged green and decorated in relief with the sign of the chemist's Santa Maria della Scala. Below the inscription engraved in the paste reads "Fece Francesco Vanni".

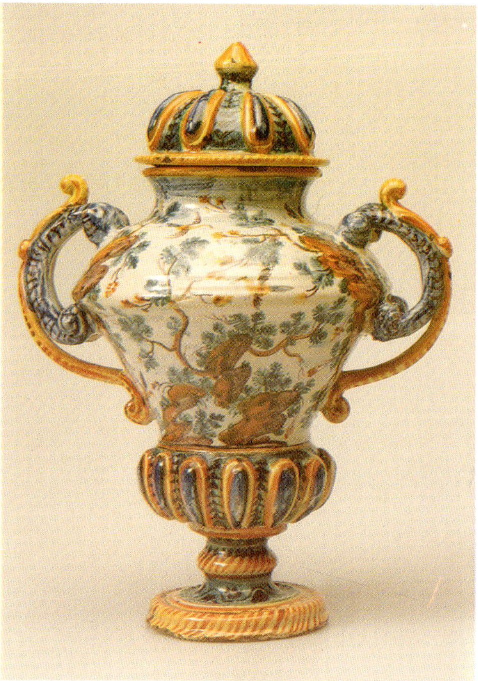

Savona, are the most famous.

Indeed, besides some examples of chemist's equipment, their workshop produced those large glossy blue plates, which, although inspired by silverware models, are quite original in the way the modelled decorations of pods, putti and shells blend with the decorative painting. Other important producers in the 1600s were the Folco, Chiodo and Ghirardi families. Nevertheless, it is still difficult to attribute works to particular factories and artists with any certainty.

At the end of the seventeenth century decorative styles develop more and more into amusing and light models. Serious historical subjects and Biblical and mythological motifs are slowly set aside in favour of rural scenes with little houses, bridges and birds in flight painted onto mainly light backgrounds. Trays and soup dishes begin to appear which are completely covered in rapid sketches which stand out against a manganese sponging. Ruins with Callot type figures are also fashionable in this period, and tend to be painted in a limited range of colours such as brown, green, yellow, and more rarely blue, although the use of plain deep blue is still found. Magnasco's rapid way of painting and the sobre choice of colours in his paintings, are the source of inspiration for many Savonese decorators in the 1700s. They produced genuine true-to-life scenes and covered the majolica, according to the prevailing fashion, with a whirl of insects, birds, charicatures and horsemen in movement which adorn plates, vases, bowls and cups.

The end of the eighteenth century is dominated by the personality of the last great Ligurian ceramics worker Giacomo Boselli who "copied everything that was in fashion in Europe" and was a real chameleon of ceramic art (Labò).

Yet he was a gifted and highly original artist, his creative talent expressing itself in the most daring inventions. It is with him that the high period of Ligurian majolica comes to an end.

VASE. Urbania, second half of the seventeenth century. Majolica baroque "baluster" vase painted in lively colours by Ippolito Rombaldotti. With the coming of the seventeenth century the ceramics centre of Casteldurante took on the name of Urbania in honour of Pope Urbane VIII.

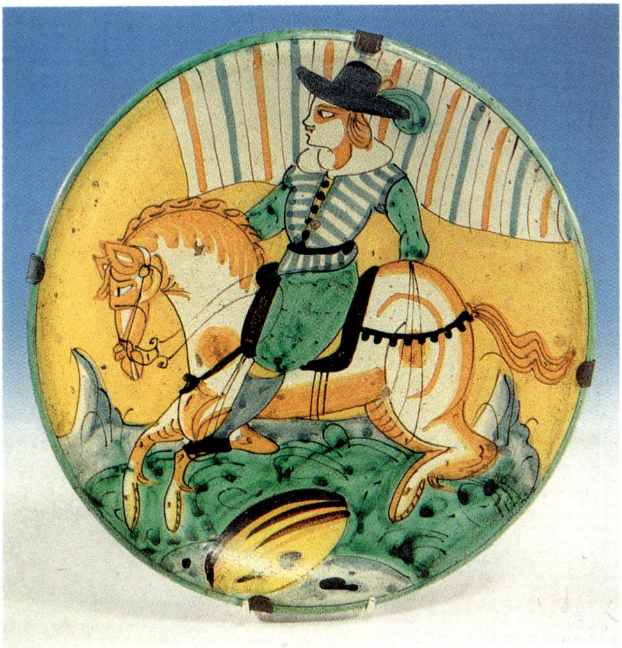

PLATE. Montelupo, seventeenth century. Plate showing soldier on horseback with a background of a mountainous lanscape partially indicated by parallel lines.

CHEMIST'S BOTTLE OR FLASK. Deruta, around the middle of the seventeenth century. Majolica with multi-coloured decoration in green, yellow and blue. In the centre there is a figure and below the inscription "aq.absiti".

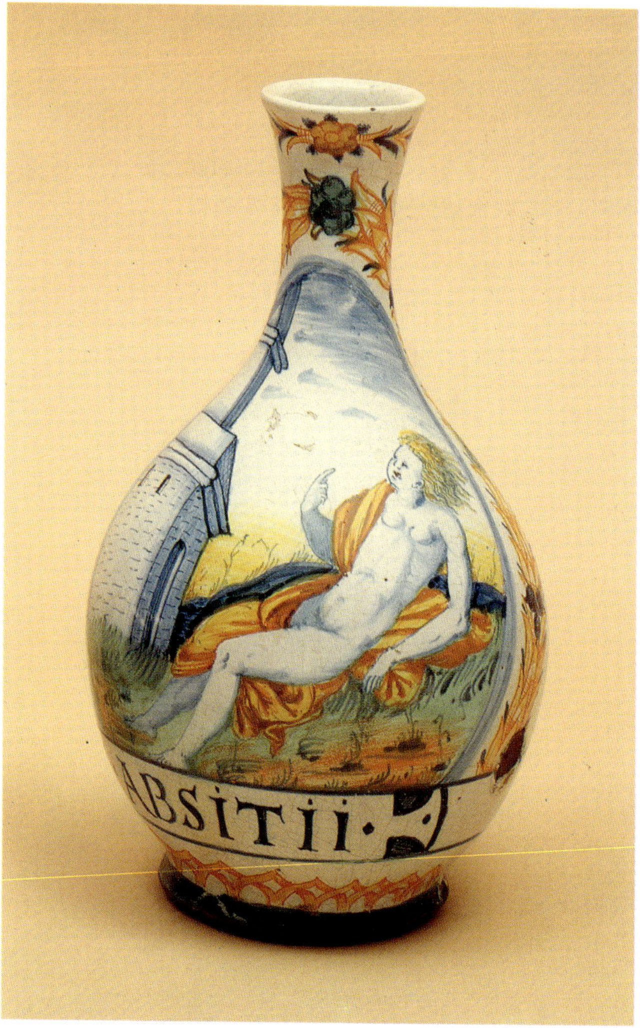

Lodi

It seems that the art of ceramics making in Lodi dates back as far as Roman times.

The first documentation, however, dates back to the fifteenth century. And at the beginning of the 1500s we hear of a potter called Cattaneo of Lodi who worked for the Gonzaga family. But it is in the

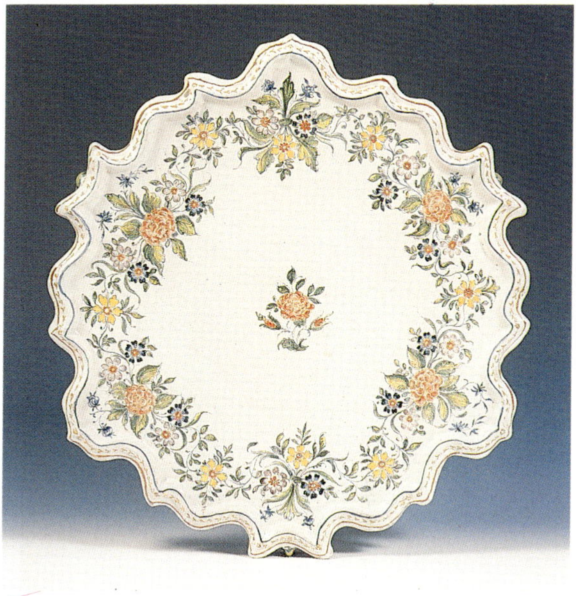

eighteenth century, as in Milan, that the most well known work is to be found and this is the work sought after by collectors.

There were many producers of majolica in Lodi but three main ones stand out. These were the Coppellotti factory, the Giacinto Rossetti works and the Simliciano Ferretti factory.

The best period at the Coppellotti factory was from the beginning of the 1700s to about 1770. This was the period when the pieces in imitation of Rouen products were created. They were decorated with geometrical motifs or chinoiserie and almost always in plain blue. Around the middle of the century we find multi-coloured decorations of flowers, landscapes, figures, fruit and fish and more rarely mythological scenes. All these operations were carried out using the great firing technique while other manufacturers had by now adopted the small firing technique, which produced a more varied and brighter range of colours.

Giorgio Giacinto Rossetti worked in lodi in the early eighteenth century. His beautiful majolica pieces, which are often signed, have decorations inspired by designs by Bérain (extremely fine decorations and delicate arabesques). Also well known in the Rossetti family are his brother Giovanni Batista and his uncle Giorgio.

CENTRE TABLE PIECE.
Lodi, eighteenth century. Multi-coloured centre table piece. In the centre a floral motif. Round the border a floreal garland, a fluted rim decorated with a continuous floral design. Six scrolled feet.

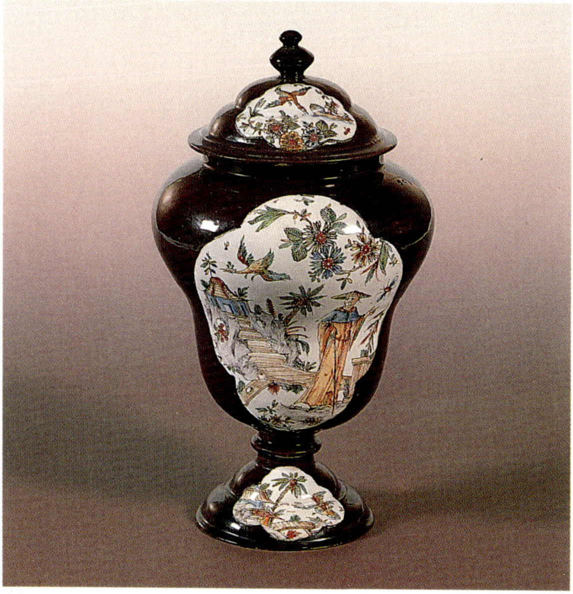

Vase withlid, Felice Clerici. Milan, circa 1760. Brown majolica vase decorated with large oriental designs on the base, body and lid.

Milano

Lombardy had ancient traditions in ceramics, but it owes a large part of its fame to its eighteenth entury majolica. And it was the workshops first of Felice Clerici and later Pasquale Rubati that created those refined pieces which are avidly collected by ceramics enthusiasts.

The prevailing taste for imported porcelain, especially in the late baroque period, forced majolica makers in Milan to follow the "new Oriental fashion" in their designs, rendering their pottery thinner so as to make it appear as close as possible to competing products. It should not be forgotten either that in the first half of the eighteenth century a great many manufacturers of fine porcelain were active in Europe and in Italy too.

The decorations used follow the prevailing taste of the period as well, with a predominance of exotic designs. The Felice Clerici factory in particular produced chinoiserie which was extremely beautiful in its stylization and use of colours.

Other ornamental motifs created by Felice Clerici are pagodas, rocks, flowers of various kinds and multicoloured Oriental flowers.

In 1756 the painter Pasquale Rubati, who was a good majolica decorator, left the Clerici works and founded his own factory. Here he produced extremely beautiful ceramics which imitated porcelain and were finely decorated in glossy paint on Chinese models, as well as on models from Meissen, Vienna and Sèvres.

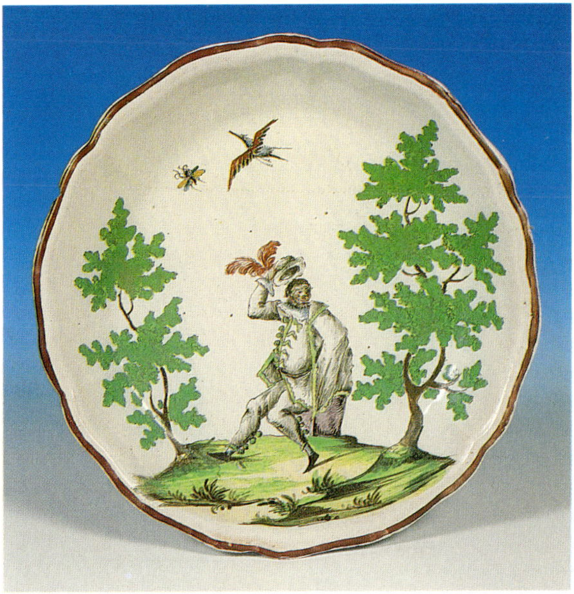

Round plate, Felice Clerici. Milan 1760. This piece of majolica has a multi-coloured decoration showing Brighella, a character in the "Commedia dell'arte". Here he hints at a dance step while removing his feathered hat. Background with trees and birds; lobate rim painted in brown.

Turin

It is only in the 1700s that Turin acquires its own tradition of majolica ware with the Rossetti family. The head of the family, Giorgio, helped by his nephew Giovanni Battista, established his own factory in 1725 and was able to obtain special privileges from Vittorio Amadeo III.

In the Rossetti factory various types of plates were produced, large trays, fruit stands, cases and soup dishes decorated with a soft plain blue and delicate, barely hinted at multi- coloured tones making his work immediately recognisable.

The decorations are similar to those of Rouen of the type called "rocaille", but Delf flowers often appear as well. They have particular forms containing figurative elements such as shepherd boys, chinoiserie and scenes of demi-gods. They are rarely religious.

Bassano and Nove

These two places are close to each other, situated at the feet of the hills near Vicenza. Between the seventeenth and eighteenth centuries a great many ceramics producers developed there.

With the closure of the Manardi factory (which happened in 1735 or 1737), the one owned by Giovanni

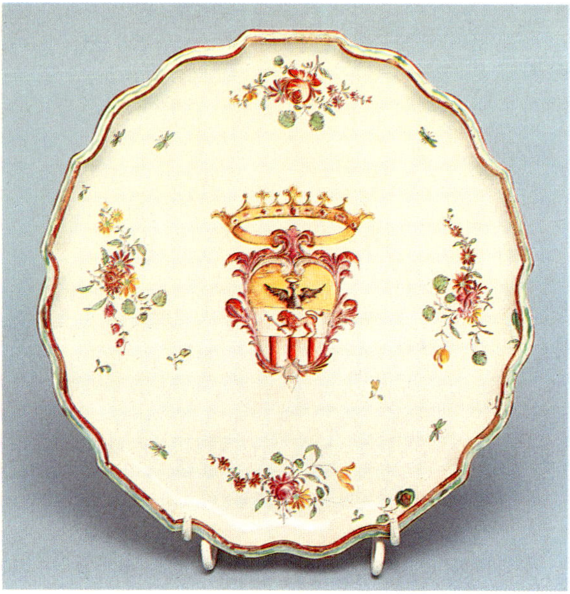

FRUIT STAND WITH SHAPED RIM. Pesaro, eighteenth century. Manufactured at the Casali and Callegari works. Multi-coloured flowery design. At the centre of the stand, the coat of arms of the purchaser.

Battista Antonibon at Nove di Bassano became ever more important. The production of "glassware" (semi-majolica shaped and painted) was abandonded in favour of majolica. In this period we find pieces which imitate Delf pottery. Antonibon died in 1738 and his son Pasquale took over his affairs. A very capable businessman, Pasquale soon made the factory a great success.

In 1752 Pasquale Antonibon began experimenting to produce porcelain, and in 1762 he was able to show a few examples to Venetian government. He then handed over the business for 29 years to one of his employees, Giovanni Maria Baccin.

The tradition at Bassano of producing plates in styles such as the "months", the "seasons", "saints" and "prophets" has made Bassano and Le Nove famous all over the world. This tradition is kept alive today, although it has no artistic or creative pretentions.

Deruta and Urbania

After its high point in the sixteenth century, the majolica produced at Deruta went the same way as that of Siena and began concentrating on the "revival" of formal and decorative models which had brought them international fame. Thus ceramic art at Deruta should be understood as a revival of classical Renaissance motifs. The technique of the metallic gloss was re-

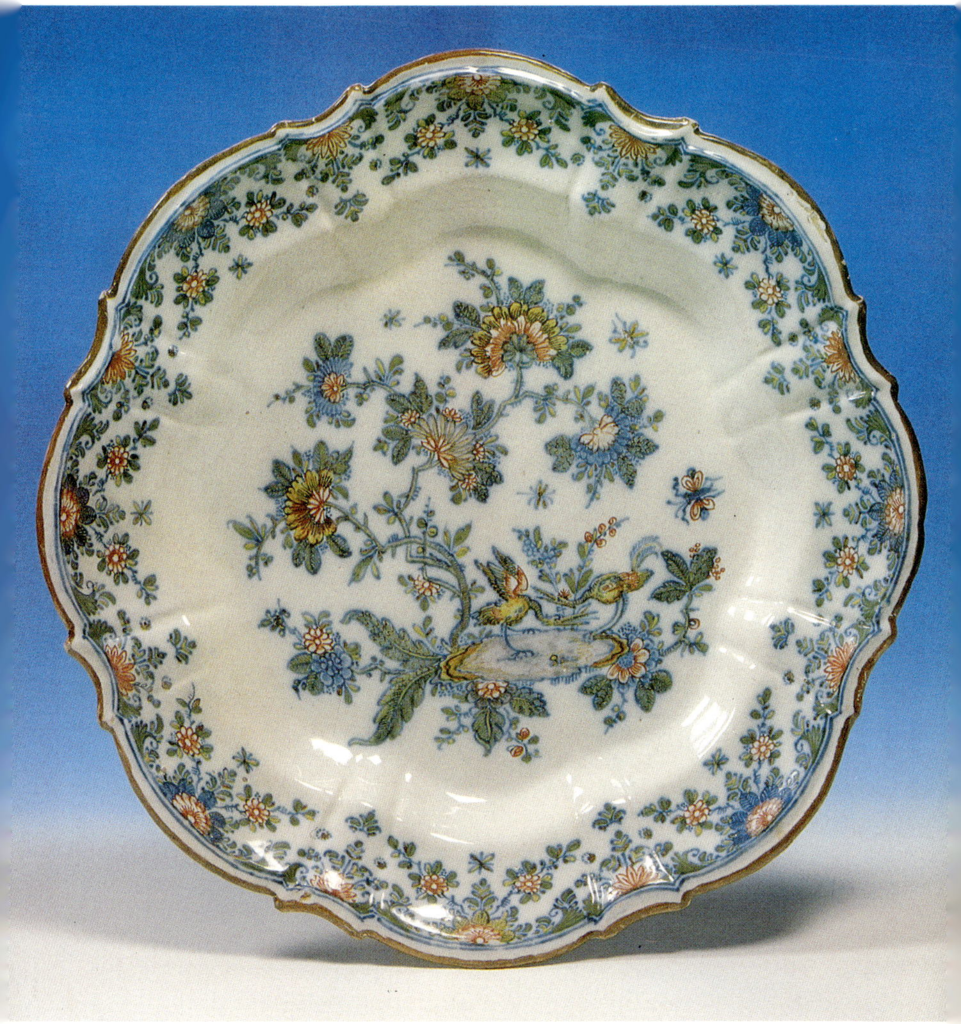

vived too, and was produced in great quantities. But at the end of the eighteenth century a "naturalistic line" style flourished which had been borroweded from Savona, but it was deeper in its tone of blue and more restrained in the sketches of hares, birds and dogs at the centre of plates, and it also employed Islamic vegetal decorations. Often the two centres are mistaken

DISPLAY PLATE. Turin, eighteenth century. A typical example of a multi-coloured design from Turin.

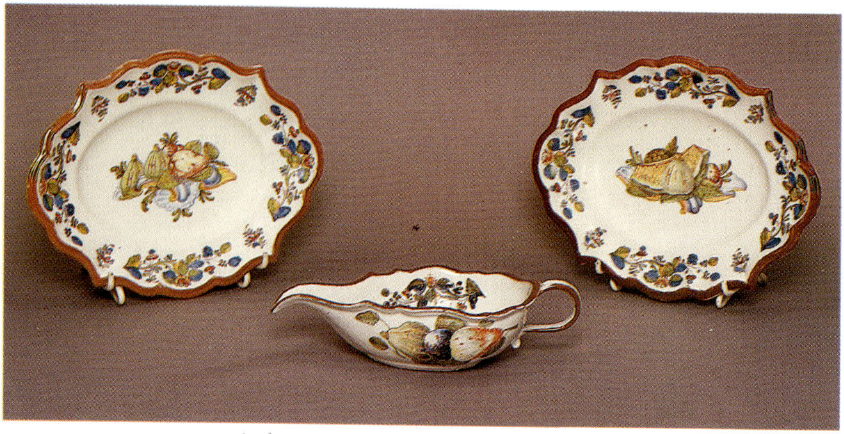

THREE MAJOLICA PIECES FROM THE PASQUALE ANTONIBON WORKS (LE NOVE -VENETO). Bassano. The pair of plates have shaped edges painted in brown. At the centre, so-called "-fruit" decoration surrounded by trailing flowers and foliage. The majolica sauce boat has an oval body and is decorated like the plates.

for each other. In order to tell the difference it is therefore wise to look carefully at the ceramic paste, at the stanniferous paint and the freedom with which the decoration is painted onto the piece.

Production at Deruta in the eighteenth century suffered a serious crisis and continued in its tired, conventional manufacture of Renaissance models.

The ancient and noble centre of Casteldurante, which in the 1500s produced majolica considered to be the best of any age, with its styles "Beauty", "Trophy", "Historical" and "Grotesque", loses a lot of its former importance in this period. Production is mainly centred around the "brief" rapid sketch kind of style and the manufacture of well made double-handled vases decorated with quick sketches in strong colours covering the whole surface. The predominant forms reflect the influence of the baroque style, as is the case with many other seventeenth and eighteenth century pieces.

Montelupo and Siena

After the high period of Tuscan ceramics in the Renaissance, in the seventeenth and eighteenth centuries production is confined mainly to Montelupo, with its popular majolica commonly known as "rough soldiers". Siena, on the other hand, went through a revival of the great sixteenth century models with "late"

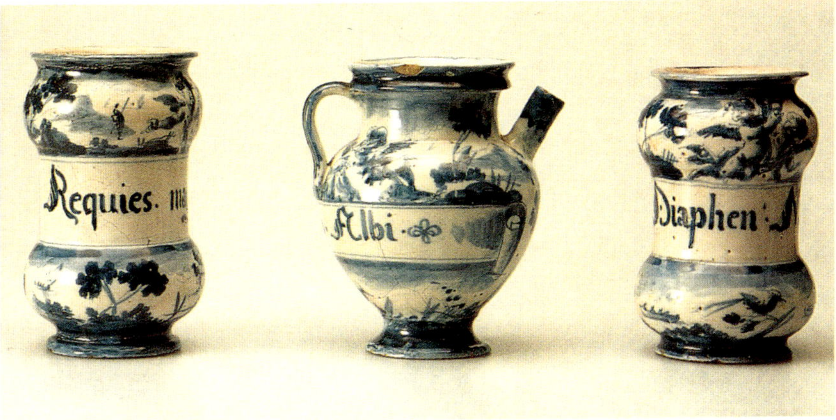

kinds of historical design, in a tired revival of Raphaelesque models.

Tuscan majolica of this period, then, is characterized by rapidly sketched figures of armed knights, painted on rather rough-looking crockery.

The colours used are intense and are dominated by a yellow background, while the soldiers, peasants and harlequins, also known as “Mostacci”, are painted in green, brown and blue.

The job of reviving the noble period of Renaissance majolica fell to San Quirico d’Orcia and to the expert majolica painter Bartolomeo Terchi. Working for the Chigi factory he interpreted scenes taken from Raffaello, Carracci and Barocci. Later in Siena Ferdinando Maria Campani revived the historical style.

It is therefore wise to be very careful when considering this type of pottery. Indeed, only an expert of the period is really able to distinguish a genuine sixteenth century piece from a mere, even if beautiful, eighteenth century imitation.

CHEMIST’S JUGS. Savona, eighteenth century. Three typically shaped majolica chemist’s jugs from Savona. Underneath the base they are marked with the star and letter “S” of the Salomone majolica family.

Pesaro

Majolica production during the Renaissance in Pesaro was quite important, but it declined and almost disappeared in the 1600s and at the beginning of the

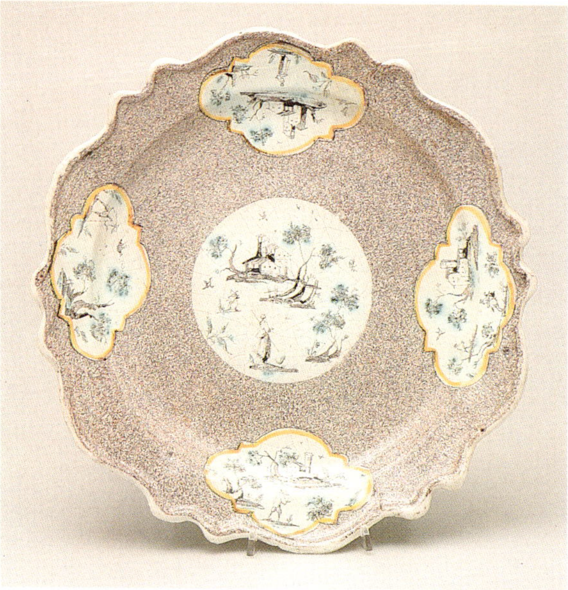

1700s. Nevertheless it flourished once again with renewed vigour in 1763 in the work of Antonio Casali and Filippo Callegari, two illustrious majolica craftsmen who came from the Feretti factory in Lodi.

The decorations naturally reflect styles typical of work done in Lodi, and they are in any case similar to the models in vogue throughout the eighteenth century at other manufacturers. Typical motifs are the rose of Strasburg, bunches of flowers, landscapes, bridges and butterflies.

DISPLAY PLATE. Angarano, eighteenth century. The centre has a multi-coloured decoration with a castle on a mountainous background. The border is surrounded by raceme foliage and painted in manganese.

On the other hand, the richness of colours employed by the partners Casali and Callegari is immediately recognizable. When they left the Ferretti works and moved to Pesaro they were already expert in using the "third firing" technique which produced more varied, lively and sharper colours. In Pesaro they developed and perfected the technique to such a degree that their work became unmistakable.

Castelli d'Abruzzo

Perhaps this is the only ceramics centre in Italy which was able to enjoy the same importance and fame it had in the Renaissance in the seventeenth and eighteenth centuries.

Already in the 1600s in Castelli we find evidence of majolica tiles in a naturalistic style showing themes taken from prints and paintings of the time. Thus a style of decorating majolica developed which was closely connected to the Flemish, Dutch and Italian painting of the period.

The golden age of this austere production, which was characterized by a use of colour similar to that of picture painting, began with the Grue family. The head of the family was called Francesco and he was the first person to look for a new stylistic direction. Then came his son Carlo Antonio, who was considered the true founder of the Castelli school of majolica. He was an excellent colourist and a creator of a new way of landscape painting which expressed an extraordinary balance between nature and the figures who were depicted.

Another eminent character in the Grue family was Carlo Antonio's son, Saverio, who continued the family tradition.

Around the middle of the eighteenth century another famous Grue was working in Castelli, Francesco Saverio. There is no doubt that no other family of majolica craftsmen had so many top quality painters as the Grue family. Francesco Saverio's work is characterized by a quick way of working and light tones. His subjects are popular ones and are taken from prints by Callot and Stefano della Bella.

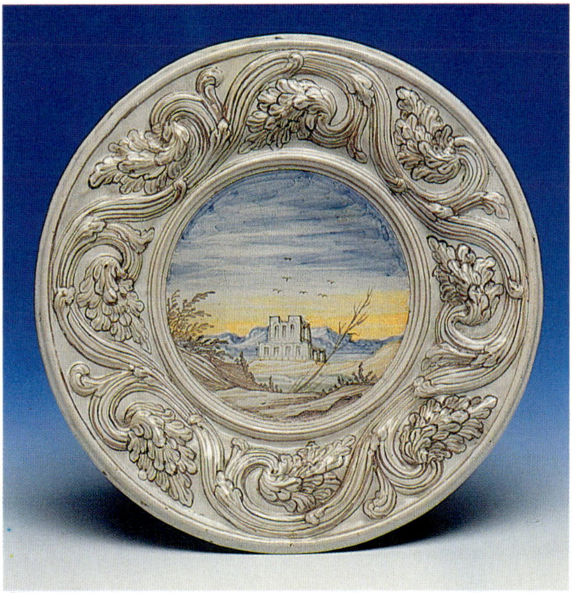

PLATE WITH A SHAPED RIM. Savona, eighteenth century. Shaped rim in the Ligurian late baroque style. This decoration known as "reserve" on a manganese sponging is quite typical of eighteenth century Ligurian ceramics.

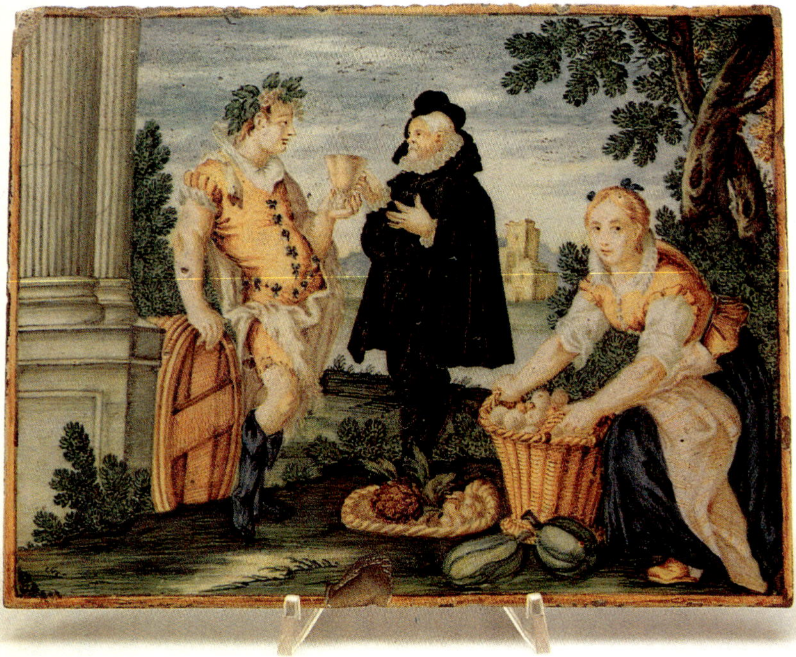